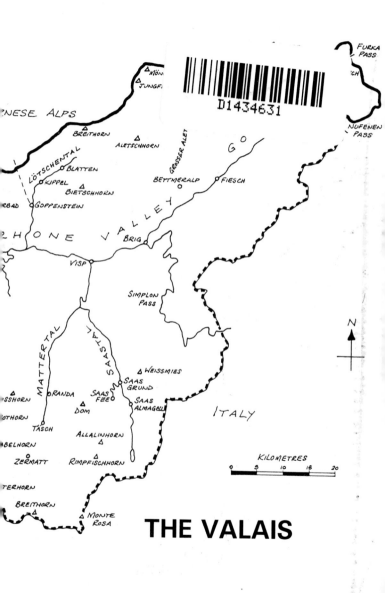

THE VALAIS

THE VALAIS
A WALKING GUIDE

The rock peak of Lo Besso (3668m) seen from Alp la Lé

THE VALAIS
A WALKING GUIDE

by

Kev Reynolds

CICERONE PRESS
HUNTER PUBLISHING INC.

First published 1989

Cicerone Press,
2 Police Square, Milnthorpe, Cumbria,
England
ISBN 1 85284 016 1

Hunter Publishing Inc.,
300 Raritan Center Parkway,
Edison N.J., 08818 U.S.A.
ISBN 1-55650-155-2

ACKNOWLEDGEMENTS

Thanks are due to a number of people whose willing assistance has helped in the production of this book. I am grateful in particular for the help and sound advice given by Herr Franz Blum at the Swiss National Tourist Office in London, to Peter Boeni of Wiler in the Lötschental, Helmut Biner of Zermatt, Dr. Daniel Fischer of Saas Fee and the staff of various tourist offices in the Valais region for their patience in answering my questions, and for giving a number of practical suggestions. I am especially thankful to my publishers for giving me the best excuse of all to spend long and glorious weeks wandering among the mountains I love. Their encouragement is very much appreciated. My brother, Alan Reynolds, drew the maps and sketches. It has been good working with him, and I'm delighted that he found time to contribute his talents to this book. Sharing the mountains, valleys, alps and glaciers at various times, and in so doing adding an extra dimension to my days in Switzerland, were Alan Payne, Derek Roberts, Claudia and Ilsa Reynolds and, as always, my wife. Their company along so many pathways is a bonus I happily acknowledge.

Kev Reynolds

CONTENTS

INTRODUCTION 7
THE VALAIS REGION 9
MOUNTAINS OF THE VALAIS 10
APPROACH TO THE VALAIS 12
TRANSPORT IN THE VALAIS 13
ACCOMMODATION 14
FLOWERS OF THE VALAIS 17
WEATHER 18
NOTES FOR WALKERS 19
PATHS AND WAYMARKS 21
SAFETY IN THE MOUNTAINS 22
GLACIER CROSSING 22
GRADING OF WALKS 24
RECOMMENDED MAPS 25
USING THE GUIDE 26

BETTMERALP
    Bettmeralp 27
LÖTSCHENTAL
    Kippel Wiler Blatten 35
SAASTAL
    Saas Grund Saas Almagell Saas Fee 49
MATTERTAL
    Randa Täsch Zermatt 75
VAL d'ANNIVIERS
    Zinal Grimentz 101
VAL d'HÉRENS
    Evolène Les Haudères Arolla 125
VAL de NENDAZ
    Haute Nendaz Super Nendaz 143

VAL de BAGNES
  Sembrancher Verbier Fionnay 147
VAL d'ENTREMONT
  Orsières Liddes Bourg St. Pierre 157
VAL FERRET
  Orsières La Fouly Ferret 165
VAL d'ARPETTE
  Champex 173

MULTI-DAY TOURS 179

APPENDIX A: Useful Addresses 184
APPENDIX B: Bibliography 185
APPENDIX C: Glossary 186

ROUTE INDEX 190

INTRODUCTION

The valley of the Rhône is a long, deep furrow cut by a plough of ice. Ice melt fills its rivers, and the big mountains that rear majestically to both north and south are laden with the permanent snows that spawn huge glaciers - among them, the largest in the Alps.

And yet the Rhône is not a frosty, arctic region at all. On the contrary, it's a warm and sunny valley, its slopes terraced with vineyards and orchards of apple, peach, pear and apricot. Its climate is more akin to that of the Mediterranean than the high Alps, and the fertility of its broad flat bed is there for all to see. But in marked contrast the valleys that slice away on either side are narrow, tight-walled and rock-girt. Tiny villages hug the steep hillsides. Above them ancient chalets and hay barns comprise alp hamlets that command some of the loveliest views in all of Europe. These views are breath-taking. They encompass shapely peaks and long ridges bristling with spires, broad snowfields and hanging glaciers and the chaos of ice-falls dazzling shades of blue in the eye-squinting light of summer. They encompass soft green pastures and the deeper forest green-that-is-almost-black, and the shadow-grey of ravines and the silver spray of cascades. Wild flowers freckle the meadows in early summer with yellows and blues and scarlet and mauve; a bewildering kaleidoscope of colour and fragrance, the air thrashed by butterflies' wings as they flit from one pollen-heavy flower head to another.

Walling these valleys, and standing sentry-proud at their head, are mountains straight out of dreams: The Matterhorn, Monte Rosa, Dom, Weisshorn, Zinalrothorn, Ober Gabelhorn, Dent Blanche, Mont Collon, Pigne d'Arolla, Mont Blanc de Cheilon, Grand Combin, Mont Dolent, Aiguille d'Argentière...the list goes on and on. Peaks, pastures and glaciers these are, that formed such a colourful backcloth to the adventures of the pioneers of mountaineering a century and more ago. On these peaks were laid the foundations of mountaineer-ing, yet one need not be a mountaineer to fall under their spell. One need not feel compelled to climb them in order to enjoy their company, for by taking to the footpaths we can bask in their glory and become for a moment part of the landscape ourselves.

The footpaths of Switzerland's alpine regions are highways to wonderland. Along them the fit and healthy, young and old, can bear witness to a world of infinite beauty that can only be imagined by those who remain car-bound. The footpaths of the canton Valais (Wallis to German-speaking Swiss) lead, surely, to some of the very best that this extravagantly picturesque country can boast. Whether your wandering is limited to valley paths, or along the mountainsides from alp to alp, or more energetically over the rugged passes that conveniently break up some of the high ridges, there will invariably be something of great beauty to see and to absorb, and thereby add a certain richness to your life.

The Valais region has its own distinctive character, be that of its mountains, its people or the architecture of its villages. It is unlike that of the Engadine or the Oberland or Ticino or the Jura. The Valais is different. You can feel it in the air. Some of its villages came late into the twentieth century. They retain a welcome simplicity that has long been lost in the bustling resorts that bear a closer kinship with European capital cities than they do with the pastoral communities nearby. But that contrast is another of the region's attributes, for there are those for whom the full comfort of home is a necessity even when abroad, whilst those who wish to submerge themselves in the culture of a peasant community that is in stark contrast to one's own background, will find plenty of seemingly lost villages in which to do so.

A 'mazot' or granary - a typical Valaisan structure

Valaisian architecture is heavily dependent upon wood. Everywhere there are the chalets of dark brown (almost black) timbers on a stone foundation standing cheek-by-jowl against the traditional *mazots* (hay barns or granaries). These *mazots* are also built of dark brown timbers, usually lengths of horizontally laid pine logs fixed one upon another as the walls that stand on stilts to resist the attention of rodents. Chalets and hay barns close ranks alongside narrow cobbled alleyways, unaltered in appearance for hundreds of years. At their windows boxes of geraniums and petunias beam out at passers-by. Here and there small squares of vegetable garden are kept trim with chard and lettuce growing in neat rows. The aroma of cut grass and cow-dung hangs over village and alp hamlet alike, while in some of the meadows women make hay dressed still in their traditional costumes of long black skirts, white blouses with black bodices embroidered with red and white threads, and with red scarves loosely tied. Some will wear traditional bonnets too, not for show, not for the benefit of tourists, but because it is simply their way.

Certain of the mountains have been sacrificed to tourism. Above Zermatt and Saas Fee, for example, cableways swing high in the air whisking visitors to remote summits where restaurants and gift shops stand on rocks that once were known only to climbers and alpine choughs. Engineers have even tunnelled through the body of one or two mountains to enable underground railways to function. Remarkable feats of engineering, maybe, but acts of unwarranted vandalism on the mountain environment.

Fortunately, such engineering developments are not experienced everywhere in the Valais, and there are scores of enchanting areas where the mountain wanderer can tread in the footsteps of the pioneers with nothing of the twentieth century to betray his vision of untamed wilderness. For although the peaks and valleys of Switzerland have all been mapped, named, measured and photographed, although their exploration has been recorded in so many different languages until it seems there is nothing left to discover, the wanderer who takes to the steeply winding trail across the alps of the Valais with his eyes alert and his senses tuned, will find many a surprise waiting just around the corner, or over the next hillside bluff.

THE VALAIS REGION

Canton Valais, third largest in the country, is that region of south-west Switzerland which surrounds the Rhône Valley. It begins at the Rhonegletscher between the Grimsel and Furka Passes, and then flows south-westwards as the valley of Goms, through Fiesch and down to Brig at the foot of the Simplon Pass. Just beyond Brig the valley swings to the west, then curves south-westward again at Sierre, which stands close by the language frontier. All to the east is German-speaking Wallis. To the west, French-speaking Valais.

The Rhône flows on towards the canton's capital, Sion. This historic town, extensively modernised and developed, has at its core a pair of castle-crowned hills that catch the eye as one approaches. Continuing, with vines on the northern slopes and orchards to the south, the river reaches Martigny, a busy town at the hub of major through-ways. To the south-west the Col de la Forclaz road winds up among more vineyards on its way to Chamonix; to the south-east runs an international highway to the tunnel and pass of the Grand St. Bernard. But the Rhône swings at right-angles, heading almost to the north now to pass the wall of the Dents du Midi before spending itself in the huge teardrop of Lac Léman - the lake of Geneva.

A fifth of the Valais is covered with glaciers. To north and south rise the largest snow ranges of the Alps: Bernese Alps to the north, Pennine Alps to the south. And it is the side valleys cutting through these mountain ranges that give the Valais its essential charm, its quality, its character, its magnetic appeal. Valleys like the Saastal, Mattertal, Val d'Ánniviers, d'Hérens, Nendaz and Bagnes and Entremont and Ferret, or northern valleys plucked out of splendour like the Lötschental. Each one - and there are others too - has its own particular blend of savage peak and soft pasture to make a visit quite unforgettable.

MOUNTAINS OF THE VALAIS

Between the Col du Grand St. Bernard and the Simplon Pass runs the chain of the Pennine Alps, and in this area there are more 4,000 metre peaks than in any other region of the Alps. Among them the highest mountain standing entirely in Switzerland (the Dom, 4,545m) above Saas Fee, and the highest massif shared by Switzerland and Italy (Monte Rosa, 4,634m) above Zermatt. This great line of peaks is a huge spawning ground for glaciers, but the largest of them all, that of the Grosser Aletschgletscher, is found not among the Pennine Alps, but north of the Rhône where it comes sweeping from the flanks of the Bernese Alps - Oberland giants like the Jungfrau, Mönch and Fiescherhorn.

The Saastal makes a grand base for a climbing holiday, as well as a magnificent walking centre. There are routes to be tried on the steep wall of the Mischabel group above Saas Fee, snow routes on Allalinhorn, Alphubel and Rimpfischhorn, and easier rock climbs on peaks neighbouring the Weissmies.

Above Zermatt most of the climbs are long routes on snow and ice.

The classic view: the Matterhorn from Findeln

There are, of course, difficult test-pieces such as the North Face of the Matterhorn, but there are easier ascents to be made by competent alpinists on peaks like Monte Rosa and the Breithorn.

Zinal, in Val d'Anniviers, is equally suitable for mountaineering as it is for mountain walking, in a valley of considerable charm. Its peaks include the Weisshorn, Zinalrothorn and Ober Gabelhorn.

Arolla is one of the best of centres for aspirant alpinists. Rising above the village are lovely mountains with glacial moats around them; Mont Collon, Pigne d'Arolla, Mont Blanc de Cheilon, each one offering interesting yet not particularly difficult ascents, while the wanderer of footpaths is treated to spectacular views from assorted alp terraces.

La Fouly, in Val Ferret, stands at the base of a line of big peaks outlying the Mont Blanc massif, and makes a quiet centre for walking and climbing holidays. Above it rise Aiguille d'Argentière, Tour Noir, Mont Dolent and the Aiguille de Triolet. Extremely steep paths wind up to remote huts perched among them; hard walking with rich rewards.

APPROACH TO THE VALAIS

Travel to Switzerland is relatively easy. Regular flights by Swissair between the U.K. and Switzerland are operated in conjunction with British Airways. Scheduled routes are from London (Heathrow) to Geneva, Basle or Zurich. Services also operate from Manchester, Birmingham and Dublin.

Air services from North America fly to Geneva and/or Zurich from Boston, Chicago, Los Angeles, Montreal and New York. Those airlines that maintain a routing across the Atlantic are Swissair, Trans World Airlines, Air Canada and Pan American.

Geneva will be the most convenient airport for visitors to the Valais. Trains run directly from that city alongside Lac Léman to Montreux, Sion, Sierre, Visp and Brig in the Rhône Valley where connections can be made with admirable efficiency via local train or Postbus to specific centres.

By rail the journey from Britain to the Valais is straightforward. Either take the super-fast TGV from Paris to Lausanne (via Vallorbe), where Valais-bound connections are made; or use the service Calais-Basle-Brig.

For those already in the Alps, there is the scenically-spectacular *Glacier Express* which runs between St. Moritz and Zermatt; or direct rail link with Chamonix via Martigny. Walkers travelling from the

Bernese Oberland have the facility of a rail link which comes from Kandersteg through the Lötschberg Tunnel to Brig.

By road there is a first-class network of motorways through Switzerland which, upon payment of a special motorway tax at the point of entry into the country, enables a fast journey to be made to the Valais. Vehicles may be carried by special trains through certain tunnels, thus avoiding a long and sometimes difficult crossing of a pass. These are the *Lötschberg* (Kandersteg - Brig), *Simplon* (Domodossola - Brig), and *Furka* (Realp - Oberwald) tunnels.

TRANSPORT IN THE VALAIS

Switzerland's public transport system is second to none. It is efficient, punctual, extensive, convenient and, for the walker, of enormous value. From a single valley base he can travel to any one of a number of locations by Postbus or train to begin the day's walk. Or, when a walk begins from the valley base and aims in a single direction along the valley or across a pass into a neighbouring valley, there will invariably be a convenient means of returning to the hotel or campsite at the end of the day.

There is a railway running through the length of the Rhône Valley offering a fast and frequent service from other parts of Switzerland. From Visp a branch line runs through the Mattertal to Zermatt - probably the busiest railway in the country.

For the northern valley of the Lötschental, a rail link is provided on the Brig-Kandersteg line via the station at Goppenstein. A Postbus ferries Lötschental-bound passengers from here to any one of the valley's villages.

Another branch line, this time running from Martigny, serves Le Châble (for Verbier) in Val des Bagnes, and Orsières at the junction of Val d'Entremont and Val Ferret. Further north, in Val d'Illiez below the Dents du Midi, a branch line runs from Monthey to Champéry.

Yellow Postbuses are seen almost everywhere there is a motorable road in Switzerland. Run by the Postal service (they also carry mail) they are as predictably punctual as are the railways. The region covered by this guide is admirably served, with practically every village having a bus route to it. In village centres the main Postbus collecting point will be outside the Post Office (PTT). In outlying areas railway stations will also have a PTT bus stop, and there are certain strategic points without habitation in some valleys where passengers may be picked up on request. Look for the PTT Haltestelle sign. Other than at these specific points, passengers should buy

13

their tickets in advance at a Post Office. By pre-purchasing tickets in this way the driver will be able to maintain his schedule.

Various incentives are available to holiday makers planning to use either rail or Postbus in Switzerland. The Swiss Holiday Card is one. Available for periods of 4, 8, or 15 days, or for one month, this ticket allows unlimited travel throughout the country by train, boat or Postbus. Enquire for details at the Swiss National Tourist Office.

Locally, in the Valais, there is a seven-day pass available for use on Postbuses within the Sion network. This gives unlimited free travel over a period of 7 consecutive days to a number of locations included within this guide. These special passes may be bought at any Post Office within the Sion Postbus area, or even on the bus itself. Similar passes are available for other local Postbus areas in the Valais. Check for details at Post Offices.

Many of the resorts mentioned in this book have assorted mechanical aids that the walker can use to his advantage; cable-cars, chair-lifts, gondola lifts etc. Where these occur, brief details are given in the text.

ACCOMMODATION

There should be no difficulty in finding suitable accommodation anywhere in the region covered by this book. The Swiss have a long tradition of hotel-keeping, and in the Valais there is plenty of every standard of lodging to meet the requirements of holiday makers no matter what their financial resources might be. Whilst one often thinks of Switzerland as being an expensive country to stay in, it is quite possible to enjoy a very fine walking holiday there without spending a small fortune. There are campsites in plenty, and Youth Hostels and moderately-priced *pensions*. There are various *matratzenlagers* or *dortoirs* (inns with dormitory-style accommodation) that would suit the pockets of those who are happy with spartan sociability, and there are the extremely grand hotels for those without wallet-restrictions. There are also, of course, hundreds of intermediate hotels and *gasthofs* and, in a number of resorts, a growing list of chalets or apartments available for short-term rent.

And there are the mountain huts.

For valley-based accommodation the tourist information office of each small town or village will be able to supply a list giving the full range available, from the cheapest to the most expensive. Swiss National Tourist Offices should also be able to give ready information. SNTO offices also stock the guide published by the Swiss Hotel

Association which gives addresses, rates, amenities etc. of some 2,700 hotels and *pensions* throughout the country. There is a smaller edition published which covers just those hotels and *pensions* in the Valais. Ask for the Valais Hotel List.

Camping: Official campsites exist in many valleys of the region. Some of these offer rather basic facilities, while others have not only first-class toilet and washing blocks, but also provide laundry and drying rooms. Do not assume that because campers are provided for in one of the larger resorts that its facilities will reflect the affluence of the area. The converse is often true! Some of the smaller, lesser-known villages take a pride in the provision of their campsites, and the holiday maker will appreciate the standards they offer. Mention is made within this book where campsites exist, but comments as to facilities provided are limited, since these may change from year to year.

Off-site camping in Switzerland is officially discouraged. Bearing in mind the limited amount of land available for pasture or making hay, this is perhaps understandable. Uncontrolled camping could do considerable damage to a peasant farmer's short season crop of meadowland hay. Above the tree-line the backpacker may find a suitably remote corner far from any alp which could accommodate a small tent for a short stay. In such cases the practice may go unnoticed or without comment. Should you choose to take advantage of such a wilderness camp, please be discreet, take care not to foul water supplies and pack all litter away with you.

Youth Hostels: At the time of writing there are several Youth Hostels in the Valais belonging to the SJH *(Schweizerischen Jugendherbergen)*, which is in turn affiliated to the International Youth Hostel Federation. Anyone holding a current membership card of the Hostels Association of his own country can therefore use hostels in Switzerland, provided there is sufficient space available. Priority is given to members below 25 years of age. Visitors wishing to take advantage of hostels in the Valais are advised to join their home organisation before setting out. Emergency international membership is possible to arrange in Switzerland, but this is far more expensive than joining at home.

Dormitory accommodation is offered in all Youth Hostels. In some, smaller twin-bedded rooms may be available, but should not be expected. Meals may be provided at some, but not all of them, and those regular hostel-users in the U.K. will be disappointed to find that self-catering facilities are not of the same standard as at YHA or SYHA hostels.

Cabane de Moiry (2825m)

Mountain Huts: Primarily huts of the SAC *(Schweizer Alpen Club)* are intended as overnight shelters for climbers preparing for an ascent of a neighbouring peak. Several walks described within these pages visit such huts as an interesting destination. Some require a very long approach, and it will be necessary to stay overnight, in which case their use by walkers is acceptable.

Those familiar with the mountain hut system in the Alps will need to read no farther, but for the first-timer a few words might be considered helpful. Firstly, mountain huts vary considerably in their standards of accommodation, if not in the basic facilities provided. In recent years a number of SAC huts have been substantially renovated, improved and enlarged. Those prospective hut users who have only read of the primitive conditions experienced in the past will be surprised by some of these improvements. But they are not evident in all huts.

Sleeping quarters are invariably of the dormitory variety; in most cases upon a large communal platform with a plentiful supply of mattresses, blankets and pillows. There is no segregation of the sexes.

If the hut is busy - and most will be in the summer season - this type of sleeping arrangement can very soon lose any attraction it might otherwise have. On arrival at the hut and finding sufficient room, it is best to lay claim to your bedspace while there is light.

Most huts have a guardian who will allocate bedspace and often provide meals. These can be either substantial in quantity and quality, or meagre and uninteresting, depending upon the interest and enthusiasm of the man (or woman) in charge. Bottled drinks are usually for sale. In some cases there is no natural drinking water available, and the guardian will sell it by the litre. Water at the washroom tap is seldom acceptable for drinking.

Staying in mountain huts is not cheap. The buildings are expensive to build and maintain, and the cost of supplying them with food and equipment is aggravated by the distance everything must be carried from the valley. Formerly carried by mule or by porter, supplies are normally brought by helicopter these days. Hence the relatively high charges made. But if you plan to undertake one or two multi-day tours in the mountains, the special atmosphere that comes from staying overnight in such remote lodgings will make the experience worthwhile.

FLOWERS OF THE VALAIS

The alpine flora of the Valais is the richest in all of Switzerland. There are a number of factors which make this so. Firstly the rocks, for there is a mixture of limestone, gneiss and schists allowing lime-loving plants to flourish in some areas, calcifuge varieties in others. Climatic considerations also play a part, as does the great range of altitude from valley bed to upper plant zone. The walker, setting out from his valley base intent on a destination a thousand metres or so up the mountainside, will pass through a number of plant zones, and it is not at all necessary to be a trained botanist to enjoy the rich variety of flowers and shrubs along the way. There are, however, several handy well-illustrated guidebooks on the market that provide at-a-glance information as to specific flowers likely to be seen. Bookshops in assorted Valais resorts stock English-language editions.

There will be all the expected varieties, from gentian to edelweiss, from alpenrose to crimson-eyed campanulas, and many more besides. This is not the place to list them all. Newcomers to the Alps may, however, be surprised to find that it is not only the meadowlands that fire with bloom, but that even the high, seemingly lifeless cliffs bordering glaciers also have their own species of flowering plant, and it is often such discoveries that make days in the mountains so memorable and rich.

A number of alpine plants are highly protected. Post Offices, some hotels and tourist information offices often display illustrated posters indicating these varieties. There are also Plant Protection Zones in certain valleys where it is forbidden to pick any of the plants. But whether protected by law or not, the best way to collect the flowers of the Alps is firstly through the senses, and then by way of the camera lens. Then others may share the pleasure they first gave you.

Those with a particular interest are directed to *Mountain Flower Holidays in Europe* by Lionel Bacon (published by the Alpine Garden Society, Woking, 1979) which has a section devoted to the Valais, giving specific areas to visit. There are also one or two commercial companies that arrange holidays in the Alps for flower-lovers.

WEATHER

Mountains make their own weather, but there are regional differences at work in the Alps that favour the holiday-maker in the Valais. In this region, south of the Rhône Valley at any rate, rainfall is less than, say, that of the Engadine to the east or Bernese Oberland a little to the north. It's also a warm region in summer with temperatures reaching as much as 25°C in the mountains, and 30°C in the Rhône Valley. However, night-time temperatures can quickly plunge - a good sign.

When the *Föhn* blows there will be clear skies for days at a time. But in the wake of this warm dry wind rain will be expected. Snow can fall at any time of the year in the higher valleys, and in early summer particularly, thunderstorms with plenty of lightning are not at all uncommon.

Weather patterns vary from year to year and it is therefore impossible to predict with any certainty as to the likelihood of arranging a fair-weather holiday. But there is some comfort in the knowledge of the Valais receives on average a better summer than many other regions of the Alps, with more sunshine, higher temperatures and less rainfall than a number of other nearby centres.

June will normally be the earliest time to contemplate a walking holiday in the Alps, and then there will be certain limitations because of the likelihood of low-lying snow and even avalanches. Late-June/early July is the best time for flowers. August is often a rather damp month, but September can be magical, though cold at night, while in October, if the weather holds, there is gold in the valleys from the larch needles turning with the night frosts, but many of the resorts will be closing down for a few weeks before the winter season begins.

Once in the Valais day-to-day weather forecasts may be obtained by telephone. The number to dial is 162. Local tourist information offices and guides' bureaux invariably display a barometer by which you can check pressure trends.

NOTES FOR WALKERS

It is to be hoped that this book will be used by casual walkers who may never have wandered an alpine valley before, as well as by the more experienced mountain wanderer aiming for the snowline. There is something in the Alps for everyone, and from personal experience I am convinced that each level has its own spice, its own very special charm. Much of the pleasure of rambling in these mountains comes from the enormous variety of scenery that the paths lead through. That variety may be experienced to some degree even in the lowliest valley, as well as upon the upper hillsides among the boundaries of heaven and earth. If the wanderer sets out with an eye for the views, for the flowers and shrubs in the meadows, the lichen-embroidered rocks beside the path, for the crystal clarity of the streams and tarns and the dark mystery of the forests, he will never be disappointed with his day.

Those who set out on a mountain walking holiday will gain most if they are in fair physical shape upon arrival. The day you begin your holiday in the Valais is not the time to start thinking about getting fit! Most regular ramblers will understand this and will have been taking walks at home before the holiday, so to avoid aching legs and a pounding heart from tackling a strenuous outing without getting the body and limbs into shape first. It is also worth remembering that some of the valley bases are still considerably higher than most city dwellers are used to, and the altitude may demand some adjustments. Don't make the mistake of taking on too much for the first day or so, but instead build up distance and height-gain steadily, day by day. Hopefully there are sufficient outing suggestions contained within this guide to enable most walkers to enjoy a good day out at any level. Certainly, every valley, hillside and ridge has its own unique flavour to sample at will.

The next point to consider will be that of equipment, the choice of which can make or mar a walking holiday. Boots, naturally, are of prime importance. They should be well-fitting and comfortable, and broken-in before embracing the Alps. Lightweight boots will see you less weary at the end of the day than the more traditional heavyweight variety. Mediumweight boots are also on the market. These will give a little more support, perhaps, for use on screes, and are likely to offer better waterproof qualities than the ultra-lightweight kind. For low valley walks along beaten-earth paths, strong shoes or trainers should be adequate.

Shorts may well be fine for most summer walks in the valleys, but upon the hillsides and higher, breeches are normally worn. A sudden breeze at 2,500 or 3,000 metres can seem extremely cold, and even the temporary loss of the sun can create a dramatic drop in temperature. Strong winds can arise almost without warning, with heavy rainfall and even snow to face at high altitudes. Be prepared with warm and waterproof clothing. At the very least a warm pullover should be worn or carried in the rucksack for low walks. Even when setting out on what is a bright warm morning, waterproof cagoule and windproof clothing should be packed, if you intend going up the mountainside. Headwear and gloves are also advisable.

If one needs to be prepared to face cold and wet weather, the extreme of dazzling sun and unshaded heat can cause problems too. Sunglasses will help those prone to headaches caused by the sun, and should in any case be taken as protection against snow glare. Sunblock or suncream should be used for skin protection. A lip salve is also useful. All these items are easily obtainable in villages in the Valais.

A small day sack should be sufficient to contain spare clothing and other necessary items such as first aid kit, map and compass, whistle, torch and spare batteries, water flask and food, on most of the outings except multi-day tours, when overnight equipment will need to be carried.

A word about drinking water in the mountains. Most of the streams seen tumbling down the hillsides should be safe enough to drink from, unless sheep, goats or cows are grazing above. I have never personally experienced any problems from drinking directly from mountain streams, but one should treat all such water sources with a certain amount of caution. Perhaps the safest course would be to limit topping up your water bottle to those hewn-out log troughs that are frequently found in valleys and pasturelands. These are filled by spring-fed pipes, and the gushing fountain should be adequately safe for drinking.

For safety's sake, never walk alone on remote trails, on moraine-bank paths or glaciers. For those who prefer to walk in the company of a group and have not made prior arangements to join an organized walkers' holiday, several tourist information offices arrange day walks in the company of a qualified leader. These take place throughout the summer and are often free of charge to those staying in the organising resort. Enquire at the information office of your village base for specific details.

PATHS AND WAYMARKS

By far the majority of paths and tracks to be followed will be routes that have been used for centuries by farmers and huntsmen going about their daily business - from alp to alp, or from one valley to the next by way of an ancient pass, or up onto a ridge where chamois might be spotted. A few have been made in comparatively recent times by the local commune, or by a branch of the Swiss Footpath Protection Association *(Schweizerische Arbeitsgemeinschaft für Wander-wege)*, by the Valais Rambling Association *(Walliser Vereinigung für Wanderwege)* or by members of the SAC in order to reach a mountain hut.

Of the officially-maintained paths there are two varieties, both of which are signposted and waymarked by paint flashes; the *Wanderweg* and *Bergweg*. A *Wanderweg* is a path that either remains in the valley itself, or runs along the hillside at a moderate altitude. These are well-maintained and graded at a much more gentle angle than the *Bergweg*. They are marked with yellow metal signposts containing the names of major landmark destinations, such as a pass, lake, hut or village, with estimated times given in hours *(Stunden* in German-speaking regions, *Heures* in French) and minutes *(Min)*. A white plate on these yellow signs gives the name of the immediate locality and, often, the altitude. Along the trail occasional yellow signs or paint flashes on rocks give assurance that you are still on the correct route.

A *Bergweg (chemin de montagne)* is a mountain path which ventures higher and is more demanding than a *Wanderweg*. These paths will usually be rougher, more narrow, sometimes fading if not in regular use. They are for walkers who should be properly equipped, for they lead to remote areas, often through rugged terrain. Signposting is similar to that for a *Wanderweg* except that the outer sections of the finger post will be painted red and white, and the intermediate paint flashes along the way will also be white-red-white. There may well be the occasional cairn to offer additional route-finding aid where the path has faded away or crosses a boulder slope, and in the event of low cloud obscuring the onward route, it is essential to study the area of visibility with great care before venturing on to the next paint flash or stone-built cairn.

SAFETY IN THE MOUNTAINS

Without wishing to be alarmist or over-dramatic, it is the duty of the guidebook writer to draw attention to the dangers that exist in mountain regions for the unwary: a sudden storm, stones dislodged from above, a twisted ankle on a scree slope etc., each of which could have serious consequences if the party is not prepared to cope with the emergency.

Wandering along a valley path should be harmless enough, but the higher one ventures in the mountains, the more realistic the walker's approach should be. Walk carefully, be properly equipped, take local advice as to weather prospects and plan your day accordingly. Take care not to dislodge stones from the path, for they may well fall onto an unfortunate walker, farmer or animal some way below. Never be too proud to turn back should you find the route takes longer than you'd expected, or if it becomes difficult or dangerous. Watch for signs of deteriorating weather and study the map well in conjunction with your compass before visibility is reduced. Think ahead.

In the unhappy event of an accident, stay calm. Should the party be large enough to send for help, whilst someone remains with the injured member, make a careful note of the exact location where the injured can be found. If there is a mountain hut nearby, seek assistance there. If a valley habitation is nearer, find a telephone and dial 01 47 47 47. This calls out the Swiss Air Rescue *but should only be used if absolutely essential.*

The international distress call is a series of six signals (either blasts on a whistle, or flashes by torch after dark) spaced evenly for a minute, followed by one minute's pause, then repeat with a further six signals. The reply is three signals per minute, followed by a minute's pause.

Remember, there is no free rescue service in Switzerland. Emergencies will be extremely expensive. Specialist mountain insurance companies often advertise in the climbing press, and some holiday insurance policies can often include mountain walking in the Alps - but check the small print for certain exclusion clauses. Be insured, and be cautious.

GLACIER CROSSING

Very few routes described within these pages venture on or near glaciers. However, a few do, so a word about ice-fields and glacier crossing might be considered appropriate.

The path from the Moiry Hut leads alongside the turmoil of the Moiry Glacier

To the inexperienced, glaciers can be exceedingly dangerous places for the unprepared. Not only the ice itself, riven as it might be with deep crevasses, but the moraine walls on either side, and the glacial slabs immediately below. All should be treated with caution. Only a very small number of glacier crossings in the Valais are considered safe for unequipped walkers. One or two are included in this guide, but enquire beforehand at the local tourist office to check the latest conditions, and if given the go-ahead, do not stray from the marked route, and keep a wary eye out for crevasses.

Since it is assumed that most walkers will not be equipped with ice axes, ropes or crampons, it should be stressed that on no account should you wander onto any glacier that is snow-covered. Should you have chosen a route that leads across one, and upon arrival find that it is so covered, turn back.

Perhaps the interjection of a personal anecdote here might illustrate the unpredictable nature of glaciers, and serve as a note of caution.

After nearly thirty years of wandering among the mountains, and with dozens of glaciers behind us, a climbing friend and I had to cross an ice-field as part of the research for this book. Our route was clear, the glacier had no snow cover, the path to the hut on the far side marked by a meandering line of red-painted cans filled with stones. There was nothing remotely about it or the day to give us cause for concern. We were well-equipped and taking standard roped precautions as we followed the line of cans. But unaccountably I felt distinctly uneasy; a feeling that only grew more intense until I was silently praying for guidance. Halfway across I just knew we had to turn back. (A difficult decision to make.) We did, in a grumble of discontent! But we'd just stepped off the ice and onto the moraine bank when there came a roar and a crash and, turning, we watched as one sérac after another toppled into suddenly-opening crevasses - where we had been just moments before. Had we not turned back when we did, this book would not have been written.

Moraine walls are composed of the broken rock and grit that have been spewed to one side by the slowly moving ice. Some of these walls, or banks, rise to gigantic proportions. Some have footpaths marked along them, but unless there is such a path, do not be tempted to climb onto them, for they can be unstable and dangerous.

Sometimes your route may lead below a glacier, and then you will be faced with crossing glacial slabs washed by the streams that flow from the ice-field above. These slabs can be extremely slippery, so do take care. Watch out also for any stones that might come clattering down, brought by the streams, or for great chunks of ice breaking away from the glacier's snout. Move carefully but quickly to reach safe ground.

But to reiterate an earlier warning: Never be too proud to turn back. If you're unsure, and there's no-one near to hand with experience to help you over, return by an alternative path. The mountains are there to enjoy, not to be threatened by.

All the above is for the exercise of caution. However, glaciers are fascinating places, and they can be extremely beautiful. Do not allow their objective dangers to lessen your appreciation of their form, their colouring or their great industry in carving the mountains and valleys into scenes of wonder. They are an integral part of the alpine kingdom.

GRADING OF WALKS

The walks in this book are designed to help you make the most of your holiday in the Valais, and since it is hoped that walkers of all degrees of commitment will find something of value contained within, it seems that a grading system might be useful to direct readers to the standard of outing of particular interest to individual walkers. Since grading is not an exact science the three categories used will cover a fairly wide spectrum.

Grade 1:   Suitable for family outings, mostly short distances involved or along gently-graded paths or tracks with little change of height to contend with.

Grade 2:   Moderate walking, mostly on clear footpaths; some will be *Wanderweg* paths, others *Bergweg* trails with some altitude gains. Walkers should be adequately shod and equipped.

Grade 3:   More strenuous routes on rough paths. Some scrambling may be involved in rare instances. There may be high passes to cross, some glacial involvement (individual routes will be marked in the text) and possibly scree work. Steep ascents and descents, and fairly long distances involved. Walkers attempting these routes should be well equipped.

RECOMMENDED MAPS

The *Landeskarte der Schweiz* (L.S.) series of maps that cover the Valais region are magnificent works of art that will breed excitement in the heart of any map enthusiast. Open any sheet and a picture of the country immediately leaps from the paper. By clever use of shading, contours and colouring, the line of ridges and rock faces, the flow of glaciers and streams, the curve of an amphitheatre, the narrow cut of a glen, the expanse of a lake and the forest cover of a hillside all announce themselves clearly. They are a source of inspiration prior to setting out, and a real pleasure to use in the mountains.

At the head of each valley section in this book, a note is given as to the recommended map to use. In every case I have chosen the 1:50,000 series, as this should be adequate for most, if not all, the walks described. (There is superb waymarking on the ground which for the most part does away with the need for greater detail than is found on these sheets.) Clearly, more details will be found on sheets at 1:25,000 scale, but rather a lot of these would be needed to cover the same area. For the southern Valais (the Pennine Alps), we are fortunate in needing only two sheets for virtually the whole area. On the original coverage, six sheets at the same scale would have been required, or about 17 at 1:25,000!

In addition, certain of the tourist information offices in the main resorts publish local sheets that are, in effect, L.S. maps with walking routes overprinted. These may well be worth studying. Ask at the tourist office for their *Wanderkarte*.

USING THE GUIDE

A brief word of explanation about this guide. Distances are given throughout in kilometres and metres, as are heights. These details are taken directly from the map, but in attempting to measure the actual distance of walks I have made the nearest estimation I could. (With countless zig-zags, it's almost impossible to be exact.) Likewise, times are also approximate only and make no allowances for rest stops or photographic interruptions. Invariably these times will be found slow by some walkers, fast by others. I make no apology for this; they are given as a rough guide only. By comparing your times with those given here, you'll soon have an idea of how much we differ! Remember though, these walks are designed for enjoyment of the full mountain experience, not for racing.

In descriptions of routes, directions 'left' and 'right' apply to the direction of travel, whether in ascent, descent or traverse. However, when used with reference to the banks of glaciers or streams, 'left' and 'right' indicate the direction of flow, ie: looking downwards. Where doubts might occur a compass direction is also given.

Finally, I have made every effort to check these routes for accuracy and it is to the best of my belief that the guide goes into print with all details correct. However, changes are made from time to time, paths re-routed, certain landmarks altered. Any corrections to keep the book up-to-date will be made in future printings wherever possible. Should you discover any changes that are necessary, I'd very much appreciate a brief note of the particular route and alteration required. A postcard via the publisher would be gratefully received.

BETTMERALP

Position:	**Situated high upon the north slope of the Rhône Valley, about 12 kilometres to the north-east of Brig, and reached by cable-car from Betten Fo (758m) on the Grimsel/Furka road.**
Map:	**L.S. 264 'Jungfrau' 1:50,000**
Base:	**Bettmeralp (1,950m)**
Tourist Information:	**Verkehrsbüro, 3,981 Bettmeralp (Tel: 028 27 1291)**

Isolated upon a sunny terrace of hillside way above the Rhône Valley, the village of Bettmeralp gazes southward over a broad panorama that contains many of the finest snowpeaks of the Valais. Along that terrace are several small lakes; Blausee and Bettmersee and one or two others without names that catch the reflections of far-off mountains and throw them on their heads. And behind the ridge that forms a natural protective wall to the village, there runs the longest glacier in the Alps, the Grosser Aletschgletscher. This comes sweeping for some 25 kilometres from the great Oberland peaks of the Mittaghorn, Gletscherhorn, Jungfrau, Mönch and Fiescherhorn. Along the walls of this great ice-field are many kilometres of footpath which give some of the most popular walks of the region.

Bettmeralp itself is a spruce, modernised resort without motorised traffic. There is no access road from the valley; visitors must either travel up by cable-car, or on foot - almost 1,200 metres in height gain! It is equally popular with skiers as it is with walkers, and as a consequence a number of mechanical aids rise above the village - cable-cars, chair-lifts, ski tows etc. One or two of these could conveniently be used to ferry visitors to points on the ridge from which to start their walks, although there's no shortage of clear paths leaving the main street.

Other access points from the valley, from which visitors may reach the high terrace, are at Mörel to the south-west (cable-car to Riederalp (1,930m) which is linked with Bettmeralp by footpath) and from Fiesch, further up-valley, which has cable-car to Kühboden (2,212m)

The Grosser Aletschgletscher, longest glacier in the Alps

and Eggishorn (2,869m), and from there footpaths go to Bettmeralp or Märjelensee. These valley cable-car stations are linked by rail and Postbus, and also have large car parks nearby.

Bettmeralp boasts access to some 50 kilometres of footpaths, and a glance at the map will give an immediate indication of the variety of outings available. Few of these, however, will be walked in solitude; Bettmeralp is in a very popular position and its fame is widely advertised. But it is well worth visiting, either for just a day or an extended stay, and its walking potential easily justifies its inclusion in this guide.

Main Bases:

BETTMERALP (1,950m) is the one main village base for walks in this section. It has hotels and apartment accommodation. (There is a Youth Hostel *(Jugendherberge)* at Kühboden, about 3.5kms to the north-east.) Some shops, restaurants, banks etc. Also tourist information office.

RIEDERALP (1,930m) stands about 4kms to the south-west of Bettmeralp and has limited facilities. Hotel accommodation. Tourist information office.

Route 1: **Bettmeralp (1,950m)-Hohbalm (2,482m)-Blausee (2,204m)-Bettmeralp**

Grade:	2
Distance:	8kms
Height gain:	532 metres **Height loss:** 532 metres
Time:	3 hours

By the use of mechanical aid (Schönbiel chair-lift or gondola lift to Bettmerhorn), the actual walking time could be considerably shortened for this outing. However, although the initial ascent section of the walk covers ground that is laced overhead with these aids, it is the approach to the high point that makes the impact of the Aletschgletscher view such an outstanding one. There are the contrasts from one side of the ridge to the other; the plunging depths of the Rhone to the south, and the sudden vista of ice-fields and great mountain walls to the north; the grass slopes and shrubbery where colours catch the sun, and a world of snow and ice and apparently barren rock. This walk is memorable for its contrasts and for the magical views.

From the cable-car station at the lower end of Bettmeralp's street, bear right and walk through the village following signs to Hotel Bettmerhorn. A broad clear footpath leads north-eastwards, passes beneath a chair-lift, over boulder-pocked pastures and comes to the white-walled hotel at a junction of tracks in about 50 minutes. *(Refreshments)*

Bear left and take the footpath heading uphill, soon to come to the western end of a narrow lake. Bear left again on a continuing path going up the hillside. This brings you to the upper terminus of a chair-lift where there is another junction of tracks and a signpost. Take the upper path (direction of Hohbalm - 50 mins) which climbs steeply in places beneath a gondola lift, and eventually comes onto the rock-strewn ridge at the rough saddle of Hohbalm (2,482m). Here we find yet another junction of tracks: the right-hand path climbs up to the Bettmerhorn gondola lift station *(refreshments)*; straight ahead to Marjelensee; left to Riederfurka and Aletschwald.

Take a few paces ahead to gain magnificent views onto the vast glacier spread before you. To the right it comes sweeping from the hidden Konkordiaplatz and the multi-buttressed Walliser Fiescherhörner, while across the glacier lovely jagged ridges rise up to the Grosser Fusshorn and Geisshorn that in themselves contain charming hanging glaciers. Snow peaks and rocky crests and ice-clad faces cluster for attention: a delightful, highly photogenic view.

The Fusshörner Ridge seen from the moraine crest above the Grosser Aletschgletscher (Route 1)

From Hohbalm bear left and wander along the footpath among boulders and shrubs of alpenroses and juniper and bilberries, along what is the very crest of the broad ridge. It is an easy, undulating path, at all times enjoying magnificent views over the Aletschgletscher. Eventually it brings you to the upper chair-lift station (from Blausee) at Moosfluh (2,333m) where there is a bench seat with a commanding view. Continue ahead for a further five minutes to find a footpath slanting leftwards with red waymarks painted on the rocks, down through a series of miniature landscapes of hillocks and hollows and shrubs, now moving away from views of the glacier, to reach a signpost at a junction of paths.

Follow the left-hand path down to the lake of Blausee, an attractive tarn in an idyllic setting, spoilt only by the intrusion of a chair-lift that transports the crowds here. It is a deservedly popular spot. Pass beneath the chair-lift and take the path down to a larger lake, that of Bettmersee (2,006m) through hillsides thick and fragrant with shrubbery. From the lake it is only a short walk back to the village of Bettmeralp.

Route 2: **Bettmeralp (1,950m)-Hotel Bettmerhorn (2,228m)-Kühboden (2,212m)**

Grade:	1
Distance:	3.5kms
Height gain:	278 metres
Time:	1 hour 15 mins

An easy, gentle walk that leads along the grassy terraced hillside with fine views ahead to a crowd of mountain peaks rising out of the Rhône's deep gulph. At Kühboden it is quite possible that you will see hang-gliders or parascending enthusiasts in action, for the hillside here makes a splendid launching pad. There is a cable-car link with Fiesch in the Rhône Valley, and another up to Eggishorn (wonderful 360° panorama) from which more walks may be started.

Walk uphill through Bettmeralp's street and take the broad footpath (as per Route 1) through pastures and beneath the chair-lift, to reach the white-walled Hotel Bettmerhorn where refreshments may be had. Continue ahead along the main path on a fairly level route. It leads directly to the assortment of modern buildings that comprise Kühboden. *(Refreshments)* A number of paths lead from here; along the hillside still to Obers Tälli, Märjelensee or Märjelewang and into the Fieschertal; steeply up to Eggishorn, or equally steeply down to the valley.

Route 3: **Bettmeralp (1,950m)-Kühboden (2,212m)-Märjenlesee (2,300m)-Hohbalm (2,482m)-Bettmeralp**

Grade:	2		
Distance:	16kms		
Height gain:	842 metres	**Height loss:**	842 metres
Time:	6-7 hours		

Another of the classic walks from Bettmeralp, this gives a fine day's walking with memorable views. Make a start fairly early in the day in order to have plenty of time to enjoy the scenery. The paths are clear and well-trodden, but there are one or two steep sections to contend with.

Follow Route 2 as far as Kühboden and continue ahead for a further kilometre until you come to a junction of paths. Take the left-hand trail which gains height up the hillside (to Eggishorn and Tälligrat). When it forks again follow the right branch to cross the Tälligrat ridge

(2,610m) which gives good views to the Fieschergletscher in the north, and descend from there to a lake (Märjela; 3 hours 45 mins) where the path divides once more. Head left on the north side of the lake, and shortly after passing its western end the path divides once more. Take the left branch which goes past a couple of small tarns and then reaches the last tarn, Märjelensee (2,300m), with the Grosser Aletschgletscher just beyond. Splendid views.

Now the path swings south to follow alongside (and a little above) the glacier for about 3 kilometres when it comes to a junction of tracks. Ahead the path continues to Aletschwald, but ours heads left and rises gradually to the saddle of Hohbalm. Over the ridge there is a choice of routes; either take the path which descends towards the upper terminus of a chair-lift and down to Bettmeralp via Hotel Bettmerhorn or, preferably, take the path heading to the right at Hohbalm along the crest of the ridge to Blausee, from where a clear path leads directly to the village. (See Route 1)

Other Routes from Bettmeralp:
A partial reverse of Route 1 takes the walker from Bettmeralp to the little tarn of Blausee, then up onto the ridge crest to join the path to Aletschwald and **Riederalp** (3 hours). This is yet another walk that exploits views onto the Aletschgletscher. Grade 2.

Follow Route 3 beyond Kühboden, then take the left-hand path which climbs steeply to the summit of the **Eggishorn** (3 hours 45 mins) for a magnificent panorama. Grade 2.

Routes from Riederalp (1,930m):
The classic walk from here involves a glacier crossing, and should only therefore be attempted by properly equipped walkers experienced in glacier travel. It goes over the saddle of Riederfurka and down onto the lower reaches of the Grosser Aletschgletscher, which it then crosses to the slopes of the Grosser Fusshorn. From here the route winds to the foot of the Ober Aletschgletscher, crosses below it and then travels along the flanks of the Sparrhorn to reach **Belalp** (2,137m). (6½ hours) Grade 3. (Add 40 minutes to this time if starting from Bettmeralp.)

The SAC (Section Chasseral) has a climbers's hut situated below the west ridge of the Grosser Fusshorn which is accessible (in 5 hours) from Riederalp. The **OBERALETSCH-HUT** (2,640m) has places for 60, with a guardian in residence from mid-June to mid-September. The route is the same as that for Belalp above, until shortly before reaching the Ober Aletschgletscher where the ways part company. Grade 3.

There are several other worthwhile walks to be had from Riederalp. Contact the Tourist Office there for details. (Verkehrsbüro, 3981 Riederalp. Tel: 028 27 1365).

Routes from Kühboden (2,212m):
There are two ways from Kühboden to the **Märjelensee**. The first crosses the Tälligrat ridge (as per Route 3 above) and takes 2½ hours. The other maintains a fairly level course along the mountainside and crosses below the ridge to reach the lake in 2 hours 45 mins. Both Grade 2.

Below Fülbärg at the junction of the Grüneggfirn and Grosser Aletschgletscher stand the two **KONKORDIA HUTS** (2,840m) owned by the Grindelwald Section of the SAC. The lower hut sleeps 45, the upper has places for 84. There is a guardian in residence from the end of March until the end of September when meals are available. Excellent centres from which to tackle a number of climbs, ski tours and the crossing of several glacier passes, these huts overlook the great amalgamation of glaciers known as Konkordiaplatz. From Kühboden the approach takes 5 hours via Märjelensee. Grade 3.

Long glacier tours starting from Kühboden (or Eggishorn) are plentiful. These include the 18 hours' classic (broken by a night in one of the Konkordia huts) to Grindelwald over the **Mönchjoch**. There is also the tour via Konkordia and over the high (3,178m) glacial saddle of **Lötschenlücke** (hut) and down to the Lötschental in 12-13 hours. Needless to say, these routes are only for experienced mountain walkers suitably equipped for glacier travel and the possibility of some ice climbing.

*Detail of wood carving illustrating the movement of cattle
to the high alps*

LÖTSCHENTAL

Position:	**To the north of the Rhône Valley, midway between Sierre and Brig.**
Map:	**L.S. 264 'Jungfrau' 1:50,000**
Bases:	**Kippel (1,376m) Wiler (1,419m) Blatten (1,540m)**
Tourist Information:	**Verkehrsbüro Lötschental, 3903 Wiler (Tel: 028 49 1388)**

The longest of the valleys draining into the Rhône from the north, the glacier-carved Lötschental is one of the loveliest of the whole region, if not in all of Switzerland.

At its head, between the Mittaghorn and Aletschhorn, dips the icy saddle of the Lötschenlücke (3,178m) from which tumbles the Langgletscher. This innocent-looking ice-field once spread itself throughout the valley and was in part responsible for scouring the deep trench that is today lush with pasture and forest. Now it is shrinking steadily back towards the saddle, while fading reminders of other major glaciers hang draped from the wall of peaks that rises on the south-eastern side.

This wall of peaks is dominated by the impressive block of the Bietschhorn (3,934m) - first climbed in 1859 by Leslie Stephen -which rises some 2,400 metres above the river. From it, to north-east and south-west, long ridges stretch out to link other summits in a formidable barrier. Below them the mountainsides are dressed with forests of larch and pine, while in the bed of the valley itself undulating meadows spread themselves above the banks of the Lonza river and beside each tidy village.

Meadows and villages alike are dotted with hay barns, but while the south-eastern mountain wall is abrupt and inhospitable, that which rises to the north-west is a bright suntrap whose slopes are adorned with pasture and woodland, and upon whose mid-levels squat several utterly delightful alp hamlets, picturesque and full of simple charm. Linking them is a belvedere footpath that will give as pleasant a day's walking as you could wish, and above one or two of these alps ancient trading passes lead to Kandersteg in the Bernese Oberland, and to Leukerbad above the Rhône to the west.

The Lötschental came late into the twentieth century. That is one of its charms. There is an air of 'unworldliness' about some of its villages; a sense of primitive antiquity aided by a folklore that has grotesque masks as its most potent symbol. These masks, carved from wood and with animal hair or fur attached, and with cow's teeth fixed to gaping mouths, are to be seen in every village; in shops or on the walls of houses. These hideous demons - *Tschaeggaettae* - appear at local carnivals where they are paraded through the village streets as they have for generations.

The road into the Lötschental from the Rhône Valley bears a sign for Goppenstein, which is the terminus for the motor-rail carrying traffic to Kandersteg through the Lötschberg Tunnel. Continuing beyond the station the Lötschental becomes a dark defile until, on reaching the first village, Ferden, it opens out and gives a glimpse of pleasures to come. These pleasures are best found by the walker, for it is only to those who take to the footpaths that the very best of this charming valley will be revealed.

Main Valley Bases:

KIPPEL (1,376m) stands little over a kilometre from Ferden, and is a most attractive village with narrow cobbled alleyways dropping steeply towards the river. Dark timbered buildings and hay barns crowd these alleys, and there are lovely views to the glaciers heading the valley. Accommodation will be found in a few hotels and pensions, while there are several holiday flats and chalets for rent. There is a campsite on the south bank of the river, reached by way of a steep and narrow road whose entrance is at the eastern end of the village. Caution should be exercised by drivers of large cars when negotiating this road. In Kippel there are restaurants, a bank and limited shopping facilities. The Lötschental Museum is situated in the village near the church.

WILER (1,419m), which stands away from the main valley highway and is approached by a short side road, is expanding faster than any other village in the valley. From it there rises the Lauchernalp cableway serving a developing ski area on the slopes of the Hockenhorn. Wiler has pension accommodation and a large number of holiday flats and chalets for rent. There are also restaurants, shops and banks, and a mountain guides' bureau. The tourist information office for the Lötschental is situated here, too.

BLATTEN (1,540m) is another attractive village, and one of the most important of the valley bases. It stands above the river with the valley road snaking away to cross to the south bank below it. There is a broad square in the village by the church, but with limited car parking space. The main car park is set below the village on the river bank. Accommodation in Blatten is in two hotels, one of which (Hotel Edelweiss), also has dormitory spaces for 38, but there are numerous holiday flats and chalets available. Basic shopping facilities are provided in the village.

Other Valley Bases:

Most villages in the valley have varying degrees of limited accommodation. **FERDEN** has pension and holiday flats; **RIED** boasts an hotel, while at **FAFLERALP**, near the end of the road, a large hotel on the edge of woods (Hotel Fafleralp) can accommodate 80 in bedrooms, and 60 in dormitories. It also has a very busy restaurant. Camping is allowed near the extensive car park at the end of the road between Fafleralp and Gletscherstafel. Facilities are minimal.

On the hillside above Wiler there is accommodation to be had at **LAUCHERNALP** - access by cable-car or by a narrow winding road - and **FIESCHBIEL**. Several chalets, holiday flats and dormitory spaces for 44 at Berghaus Lauchern, and 23 at Restaurant Zudili.

Postbuses serve each village in the valley. They run frequently throughout the summer as far as the large car park at the end of the road.

Mountain Huts:

Two SAC huts are accessible from the Lötschental. These are the **BIESCHHORN HUT** (2,565m), owned by the Akademischer Alpenclub of Bern; and the **LÖTSCHEN HUT** (3,238m) perched a little above the Lötschenlücke and in the care of the Bern section of the SAC. This has room for 106 and is ideally placed for ski tours on the Grosser Aletschgletscher which flows virtually from its door, and for the traverse of several neighbouring peaks. It has a guardian in residence from 1st April until the end of May, and from July to the end of August. Accessible in about 7 hours by way of the Langgletscher.

The Bieschhorn Hut is, as its name suggests, situated under the peak of the same name, and is reached in about 3½ hours from either Wiler or Blatten. The hut can sleep about 40 in its dormitories, but it has no resident guardian.

Elsewhere there is the **LÖTSCHENPASS HUT** (2,690m) on the col leading to the Gasterntal (for Kandersteg). This hut is reached in 2

Bietschhorn (3934m) from the Lötschentaler Höhenweg

hours 15 mins from Kummenalp above Kippel and offers overnight dormitory places and refreshments, while at **KUMMENALP** itself (2,083m) there is a Gasthaus with both bedrooms (11 beds) and dormitories (30 spaces).

Route 4:	Ferden (1,375m)-Faldumalp (2,037m)-Kummenalp (2,083m)-Lauchernalp (2,106m)-Fafleralp (1,787m)

Grade:	2
Distance:	18.5kms
Height gain: 731 metres	**Height loss:** 319 metres
Time:	6½-7 hours

This is the classic walk of the valley; the *Lötschentaler Höhenweg*. It is one of the loveliest walks in the Valais, a truly delightful outing with picturesque views all the way. Although not at all difficult, it is given a Grade 2 here on account of its length and the steepness of the path leading from the valley to Faldumalp. However, many ramblers break this outing into two separate walks, and make use of the Lauchernalp cableway to relieve the effort of the initial climb up the mountainside. This alternative method of tackling the walk is offered below as Routes 4a and 4b - both graded 1.

There are several aspects of this walk that would alone be sufficient to give it classic status. There are the views, to begin with. Views that burst over the whole valley and reveal its full glory in a single glance; views that insist on raising the walker's eyes to the splendour of the Bietschhorn opposite - or way back to the south, far beyond the hinted depths of the Rhône Valley, to Monte Rosa and many other giant snow peaks worrying the horizon. There are the alp hamlets - eight of them - that enliven the route with their interest and variety. There is the path itself, a splendidly graded trail that undulates along a vague terrace of hillside, in and out of the shade of trees, cutting back here and there to cross a tumbling stream, climbing now and then to cross a green bluff, passing over meadow belvederes far above the valley.

There are several opportunites along the route to descend to the valley, should you decide at any time to foreshorten it. A truly grand walk.

It begins in the village square of Ferden. The square is set by the church and a signpost directs the route leftwards to Faldumalp. You

Faldumalp, overlooking the Lötschental

are soon above the village where another signpost points along a path climbing among trees and steep grassy hillsides. *(The Höhenweg waymark is a yellow diamond with black edging, and is found painted on trees, rocks, haybarns etc.)* This path gains height rapidly on steep windings, and when it emerges from forest to pastures, rewards with spectacular views to the head of the valley. In 1½ hours the path reaches the glorious little alp hamlet of Faldumalp with its tiny chapel overlooking the depths of the Lötschental.

Retrace the approach path for a short distance back to its crossing of the Faldum stream where the path divides. Now take the left-hand option towards Restialp. This is a splendid belvedere section, narrow and a little exposed in places, that goes among larches and slopes of bilberries and alpenroses. Just below the hamlet of Restialp you come to a junction of tracks. Take the path heading left up the slope to the alp hamlet (2,098m) where refreshments are available.

The path continues to Kummenalp (in 30 minutes), always with fine views. Kummenalp has refreshments and a Gasthaus with beds and dormitory places. Behind it there's a bowl of green pastureland with streams rushing through, and a high path leading up to the Lötschen-pass beyond which (6 hours 45 mins away) lies Kandersteg.

From Kummenalp the *Höhenweg* maintains its journey of delight to Hockenalp (in 40 minutes), with views dominated by the Bietschhorn. Hockenalp (2,048m) is a little cluster of timber chalets and hay barns *(refreshments)*, and the path continues beyond it over neatly shorn hillsides seething with crickets, rich in wild flowers early in summer, to reach the slopes of Lauchernalp in twenty minutes. (Possibility here to descend to Wiler in the valley by cable-car.) Lauchernalp has various ski tows and chair-lifts running across its open bowl of hillside. It also has refreshments and accommodation.

The continuing path descends a little (follow waymarks), then traverses the hillside to Weritzalp (Weritzstafel - 2,099m) in a further 45 minutes. This hamlet is a huddle of red-shuttered chalets *(refreshments)*, and beyond it the route begins to slope down through forest trees to the few hay barns and alp huts of Tellialp (Tellistafel -1,865m) in 1 hour 40 minutes. Then it crosses a stream and follows an undulating course round the hillside, passes the little tarn of Schwarz-see and comes to Fafleralp *(refreshments, accommodation - and a superb modern chapel in the woods behind the hotel)*. In ten minutes from Hotel Fafleralp the path comes to the large car park at the end of the valley road. (Postbus)

Route 4a: **Lauchernalp (1,922m)-Kummenalp (2,083m)-Restialp (2,098m)-Faldumalp (2,037m)-Ferden (1,375m)**

Grade:	**1**
Distance:	**10.5kms**
Height gain:	**176 metres** **Height loss:** **723 metres**
Time:	**3 hours 40 mins**

By judicious use of the cable-car from Wiler to Lauchernalp, the *Lötschentaler Höhenweg* can be divided into two separate outings. This is the westward route, a walk of great charm (see introductory paragraphs to Route 4 above) that links several alp hamlets and delights in spectacular views. Refreshments are available in each of the hamlets, save that of Faldumalp. The waymark for this route is a yellow diamond with black edging. These, and signposts at strategic footpath junctions, ensure that the walker cannot miss the way. The path is easily graded and well maintained. Its steepest sections are to be found on the final leg from Faldumalp down to Ferden in the valley. Postbuses serve Ferden, and will conveniently transport you to your valley base at the end of the walk.

Route 4b: **Lauchernalp (1,922m)-Weritzalp (2,099m)-Tellialp (1,865m)-Fafleralp (1,787m)**

Grade:	**1**
Distance:	**8 kms**
Height gain:	**177 metres** **Height loss:** **312 metres**
Time:	**2½ hours**

The eastern section of the *Lötschentaler Höhenweg*, this is the least taxing of the high routes, but it is nonetheless a worthy outing. Take the cable-car from Wiler to Lauchernalp, then head off to the right along the waymarked footpath, enjoying the views and the alp hamlets along the way. For details, see the latter part of Route 4's description.

Route 5: **Ferden (1,375m)-Faldumalp (2,037m)-Niwen (2,769m)**

Grade:	**2**
Distance:	**6kms**
Height gain:	**1,394 metres**
Time:	**4½ hours**

The summit of Niwen offers a rewarding panorama overlooking all the

Lötschental to the north-east, and the Rhône Valley and great snow peaks of the Pennine Alps to the south.

Take Route 4 (above) as far as Faldumalp where a signpost by the church directs the continuing path above the hamlet. It is a clear path for most of the way, and no difficulties should be encountered. Allow 2½ hours from Faldumalp.

Route 6:	Ferden (1,375m)-Restialp (2,098m)-Restipass (2,626m)-Torrentalp (2,459m)-Leukerbad (1,401m)

Grade:	2-3	
Distance:	15kms	
Height gain:	1,251 metres	**Height loss:** 1,225 metres
Time:	6-7 hours	
Additional map:	L.S. 5009 'Gstaad-Adelboden'	

A classic crossing, this offers a most interesting day's walking with some spectacular views. There will be plenty of overnight accommodation to be had in Leukerbad, and a return to the Lötschental can be arranged by a combination of Postbus and railway.

From Ferden a signposted track swings in long loops up the hillside - footpath short cuts give alternatives here and there - and takes you directly to the little alp hamlet of Restialp *(refreshments)*. An attractive valley cuts away behind the hamlet with a footpath, signposted to Restipass and Leukerbad, leading through it to the saddle at its head. (1 hour 20 mins from Restialp.)

Continuing down on the western side of the Restipass with views to the big snow peaks to the south of the Rhône, the route leads to the lake of Wysse See, (a rich area for alpine flowers) trapped in a bowl of mountain, and on to Torrentalp (2 hours from the pass; *refreshments*). It is possible from this point to shorten the walk by taking the cable-car down to Leukerbad - a saving of more than 1,000 metres and nearly 2 hours of descent. Keen walkers, however, will continue on the waymarked path down to the village.

Leukerbad is a popular spa and winter sports resort set in a sun-trap of an amphitheatre below the Gemmi Pass, and linked with the Rhône Valley by 15kms of road.

Route 7:   **Kummenalp (2,083m)-Lötschenpass (2,690m)-
              Kandersteg (1,176m)**

Grade: **3**
Distance: **15kms**
Height gain: **607 metres**   Height loss: **1,514 metres**
Time: **6 hours 45 mins**
Additional map: **L.S. 5009 'Gstaad-Adelboden'**

Crossing the Lötschenpass one leaves the canton Valais and enters the
Bernese Oberland. It's a fine outing; an historic passage and a popular
one. There are no major difficulties and the grading is on account of
its length - and the fact that a glacier has to be tackled on the descent.
(The route is marked, but beware after fresh snow.) Accommodation
is available at Kummenalp, Lötschental Hut, Gfällalp (matratzenlager), Selden (hotel) and Kandersteg (camping, hotels, matratzenlager etc.). Return to the Lötschental by train through the Lötschberg
Tunnel to Goppenstein.

   If the plan is to start the walk from Ferden or Kippel, add 2 hours to
the total walking time. Alternatively, take the cable-car from Wiler to
Lauchernalp and find the Lötschenpass direct route avoiding
Kummenalp. (15 minutes longer than Kummenalp - Lötschenpass.)

   At Kummenalp a clear, signposted trail leads into the hanging valley
behind the hamlet and heads up rough slopes and past a few little tarns
to reach the pass (2 hours 15 mins; *refreshments*). However, before
coming onto the pass, stop to admire the magnificent views
overlooking the Bietschhorn a little south of east, and far off to the
Mischabel group, Weisshorn and Monte Rosa gleaming in the sun. At
the Lötschenpass the northward view looks to the Doldenhorn rising
above the Gasterntal, and north-east to the Blümlisalp.

   On the Oberland side of the pass the way descends a little, then goes
down the right-hand side of the Lötschengletscher. The route is
usually marked in summer and is fairly obvious. From the foot of the
glacier the path heads over moraine debris to the Gfällalp (*refreshments*). Down then, alongside the glacial stream to the valley bed, and
across to the hamlet of Selden (4 hours 15 mins from Kummenalp;
refreshments). Bear left and wander down the valley road for about 5.5
kilometres to reach Kandersteg.

   Kandersteg is a busy little resort with all the usual amenities for
summer and winter visitors. Plenty of accommodation of varying
standards; restaurants, shops, banks, PTT etc.

Route 8:   Fafleralp (1,787m)-Krindeln (Chrindellun) (2,230m)

Grade:	**2**
Distance:	**4kms**
Height gain:	**443 metres**
Time:	**1½ hours**

A relatively short walk, this could make good use of half a day with some fine rewarding views to be had from the high point. It begins at the car park at the north-eastern end of the valley, and from there heads back towards a tree-clothed bluff by crossing a bridge and bearing right along a broad track. Follow the track as its swings to the left, and shortly after bear right where it forks. This brings you to the hamlet of Fafleralp by a small pond. (Signpost here for Krindeln.)

The way now heads off to the right and enters larch woods. Climbing easily by way of lengthy zig-zags, the route gains height above the Inners Tal, becomes a little steeper and brings you to a lovely grassy knoll (avalanche fences) offering magnificent views to the snowy saddle of Lötschenlücke to the east, of the main valley sweeping away below, and across to the wall of peaks dominated by the Bietschhorn.

Route 9:   Fafleralp (1,787m)-Gugginalp (2,108m)-Fafleralp

Grade:	**1**		
Distance:	**8 kms**		
Height gain:	**321 metres**	**Height loss:**	**321 metres**
Time:	**2 hours 45 mins**		

An undemanding yet enjoyable tour of the head of the valley, this walk wanders through rough meadowlands below the Langgletscher. There are glacial streams, little tarns, larch woods and hillsides bright with shrubbery, and the basic alp hamlets of Gletscherstafel and Guggistafel along the way. It's an outing not likely to be trod in solitude, especially the initial stretch on leaving the car park which is invariably busy. It is, however, an ever-varied walk with opportunities for the inquisitive to explore areas a little off-trail.

Leave the car park at the head of the valley (*refreshment kiosk*, toilets, Postbus stop) and head through the gate leading up-valley on a footpath marked to Grundsee, Gletschertor, Ananensee and Guggistafel. The path leads through pastures with the chalets and hay barns of Gletscherstafel seen off to the left, and glaciers ahead. Cross a bridge over the stream and bear left along a well-worn footpath that winds uphill to cross another stream, after which you bear half-right and come to the green tarn of Grundsee - a popular picnic site. Continue beyond the tarn heading through boulder-pocked pastures and open meadows. The path becomes indistinct among a slightly marshy area (cotton grass) where you veer half-left to join another path (red and white paint marks) leading up-valley. At the end of the meadowland the way climbs between stands of larch in full view of the Langgletscher; it crosses through a rough boulderscape and, shortly before the glacier's snout, heads left over a substantial bridge spanning the glacial torrent.

Now on the north side of the valley continue to gain height over a wild and unlovely hillside strewn with boulders that suddenly gives way to slopes of alpenroses (afire with bloom in early summer) and dwarf alder, and this in turn is exchanged for soft springy turf in a splendid glacial cwm at the entrance to the Jegital. Ahead now views offer the Lauterbrunnen Breithorn rising above the Jegi Glacier. With the glacial stream pouring down to your left you come to a junction of three paths - all marked with white-red-white paint splashes! There is no signpost, but the path directly ahead leads up to the glacier; that which branches right goes to the little tarn of Ananensee (a fine viewpoint); and ours heads left.

Cross the glacial stream on a footbridge (note the mini-gorge directly beneath, carved by the force of the water) and follow the path back to Fafleralp. It leads through pleasant pastures, beside the Guggisee (another tiny tarn) and goes below the alp hamlet of Guggistafel through an area of shrubs and larches, and back to the car park.

Route 10:	Fafleralp (1,787m)-Petersgrat (3,206m)- Kanderfirn-Kandersteg (1,176m)

Grade:	3	
Distance:	18 kms	
Height gain:	1,419m metres	**Height loss:** 2,030 metres
Time:	11 hours	
Additional map:	L.S. 5009 'Gstaad-Adelboden'	

This long, demanding day's journey should only be attempted by those familiar with glacier crossings as much of the route lies over snow and ice-fields. It is essential, too, that the necessary equipment for safe travel over glacier terrain be taken. There are no major difficulties, but caution should be exercised at all times. Note that there is a hut *(Mutthorn Hut 2,898m, 100 beds, guardian from end of June to late September, meals and drinks provided)* situated on a rocky promontory to the south-east of the Mutthorn and about 100 metres below the snow saddle at the head of the Kanderfirn Glacier (east side). Make an early (pre-dawn) start in order to avoid the worst effects of the sun on the glaciers.

From the little pond at Fafleralp (see Route 8 above) take the track left which gains height and swings round into the mouth of the Uisters Tal (also known as the Äusseres Faflertal). On reaching the stream leave the main track and take to the path leading into the valley along the east bank (true left bank). At the head of the valley it climbs steeply to the north of the Krindelspitz where you gain the Üssertal Glacier with the long snow ridge of Petersgrat directly above. Make for the lowest point on the ridge a little west of north from the point at which you joined the glacier. The broad flat Petersgrat arête presents magnificent views in all directions, but particularly of the big peaks of the Valais to the south, across to the Bietschhorn guarding the Lötschental, and of Blüemlisalp ahead.

Now descend the easy glacier heading due north towards the saddle below the Mutthorn. *(The hut is found a short distance below this to the right.)* From the saddle views take in the west face of the Jungfrau. Bear left and go down the Kanderfirn Glacier keeping to its left-hand side, and when you reach the end of the ice-field you should come to a marked path which leads steeply down to the Gasterntal. Once in the valley *(refreshments at Selden)* follow the road for 5.5kms to Kandersteg.

Kandersteg has a variety of accommodation and all facilities. To return to the Lötschental take the train through the Lötschberg Tunnel to Goppenstein where Postbus may be caught to your valley base.

Route 11: **Fafleralp (1,787m)-Blatten (1,540m)-Goppenstein (1,216m)**

Grade:	1
Distance:	13 kms
Height loss:	571 metres
Time:	3 hours

What a pleasant, gentle stroll this is; the sort of outing that is ideal for families with young children to take a whole day over, picnicking on the way, taking time out to study flowers or to stray to villages for refreshments and variety. And should you at any time decide to shorten it, there will always be a convenient crossing to one of the valley's villages that is served by Postbus to take you back to your base. An easy walk on mostly clear paths; full of fragrance in summer, rich with wild flowers early in the season, golden with the autumn tints of larches in late September and October.

From the car park at the head of the valley (Postbus) take the track to the hamlet of Fafleralp on the right bank of the Lonza river. A signpost here directs the route down-valley on a clear path to Eisten, and shortly after to Blatten *(refreshments)*. From here go down below the village to cross the river where a footpath on the left bank leads through pastures and woodland patches, past attractive hay barns and alp hamlets all the way to Goppenstein. Cross here to the right bank for the Postbus back into the main valley.

In the square at Saas Fee stands Johann Imseng, (1806-69), priest, hotelier and mountaineer who did more than anyone to promote the valley as a true mountain centre.

SAASTAL

Position:	**South of the Rhône Valley, approached from Visp.**
Map:	**L.S. 5006 'Matterhorn-Mischabel' 1:50,000**
Bases:	**Saas Grund (1,559m) Saas Almagell (1,673m) Saas Fee (1,809m)**
Tourist Information:	**Verkehrsbüro, 3901 Saas Grund (Tel: 028 57 2403) Verkehrsbüro, 3905 Saas Almagell (Tel: 028 57 2653) Verkehrsbüro, 3906 Saas Fee (Tel: 028 57 1457)**

The Saastal (Saas Valley) owes its popularity to the pioneers of mountaineering who, a century and more ago, were drawn here by the magnificent array of peaks curving in a dazzle of ice and snow above Saas Fee, by the huge steep wall of the Mischabel group that separates the valley from that of Zermatt (containing among its summits the Dom, at 4,545m the highest mountain entirely in Switzerland), and by the glacier passes near the head of the valley by which access with Zermatt to the west was made not only possible, but scenically spectacular.

Yet long before these mountains became part of the 'Playground of Europe', the Saastal was for centuries on an important trade route that crossed into Italy by way of the Monte Moro or Antrona passes. The first of these, at the very end of the valley above the Mattmark lake, has been in use since at least the 13th century, and it descends to Macugnaga in full view of the vast east face of Monte Rosa; while the Antrona Pass links the Furggtälli (cutting south-east of Saas Almagell) with that of the quiet Valle d'Antrona that flows down to Villadossola and the Italian lakes.

The ancient mule trail of the Saastal which for hundreds of years enabled access with the outside world, was not replaced with a motor road until the 1930's (it was 1938 before it reached Saas Grund), while the first cars laboured to Saas Fee only in 1952. But while the valley

took a long time to be 'opened up' to the outside world with an easily accessible road, there was an hotel at Saas Fee as long ago as 1850 in recognition of the enormous potential for tourism here. And today one need only pause for a moment to appreciate the natural attractions of the valley that are surely no less than those known to the pioneers.

Entering from Visp the visitor approaches for 7 kilometres along the

MONTE ROSA.

BREITHORN

ZERMATT

MATTERTAL

Vispertal which forks at the village of Stalden. The western branch goes up to Zermatt, the eastern (left fork) becomes the Saastal. It is a narrow, rock-girt valley at first, (Saas comes from the Italian *sasso* which means rock) the road clinging to the mountain wall some way above the river as it squeezes through Eisten and Huteggen, but at Saas Balen the valley begins to open out with prospects of dramatic peaks beginning to display themselves ahead. In another 4 kilometres the road reaches Saas Grund at the foot of the Weissmies (4,023m) and Lagginhorn (4,010m), formerly the most important of the Saas villages but now rather overshadowed by the magnetic jewel of Fee.

Beyond Grund the valley continues towards the south, narrowing on the approach to Saas Almagell that has a brace of minor valleys projecting away from it into the eastern wall of mountains. South of Almagell the Saastal opens once more to the large dammed lake of Mattmarksee into which drain the glaciers streaming from the frontier ridge. This lake, now safely contained by a huge wall, was responsible in the past for a series of disastrous floods that caused devastation to buildings and the deaths of many villagers when it burst its moraine banks. Even during the construction of the barrage in 1965, 88 workmen lost their lives when a mass of ice from the overhanging Allalin Glacier crashed down on their site.

Above Grund to the south-west sits Saas Fee, approached by a fine road that climbs in two long loops through the forest to emerge into the sunny bowl of an amphitheatre scooped out long ago by the great ice-fields that hang so dramatically from the wall of peaks ahead. Those peaks are, from left to right; the snow dome of Allalinhorn (4,027m), then the saddle of Alphubeljoch which rises to the flattened crest of Alphubel (4,206m); the sharp rock wall of Täschhorn (4,491m), followed closely by the Dom (4,545m), Lenzspitz (4,294m) and Nadelhorn (4,327m). It is a magnificent collection of peaks, compelling to the climber interested in routes of a classical nature, while the mountain walker has a wonderland all his own to explore with those shining summits creating a backcloth to dreams.

Main Valley Bases:
SAAS GRUND (1,559m) nestles in the valley below the Weissmeis on the right bank of the river. Originally the main village of the Saastal, its old traditional buildings have become outnumbered by those of more recent construction built to house a growing number of visitors in both winter and summer. There are plenty of hotels and apartments, and several campsites offering accommodation at both ends of the spectrum. Saas Grund has a helpful tourist information office, adequate shopping facilities, restaurants, banks, PTT, a climbing school and a gondola lift operating (summer and winter) to Kreuzboden and Hohsaas on the slopes of the Weissmeis.
SAAS ALMAGELL (1,673m) is the last of the villages in the valley. Smaller than Grund, it nevertheless has a number of hotels of one, two and three star ratings. There are also restaurants, a tourist information

*Täschorn (4490m), Dom (4545m) and Lenzspitze (4294m)
above Saas Fee*

office and limited shopping facilities, and a chair-lift to the alp hamlet of Furggstalden.

SAAS FEE (1,809m) has expanded in size and facilities at a very rapid rate in recent years, yet somehow has managed to retain the character of a true mountain village without being totally submerged by its international appeal. Few alpine villages have a more dramatic setting, and the mountain walker will not run short of outings of great charm in and around the glacial amphitheatre that embraces it. Motor vehicles are not allowed in the village; parking is in a huge open-air car park, or in the Parkhaus at the entrance to the village. There is no shortage of hotel, chalet or apartment accommodation. There is a Youth Hostel and a simple campsite (no caravans). The village streets are lined with shops and stores offering everything from ice creams to extravagantly expensive watches. There are banks and restaurants, a tourist information office, mountain guides' bureau, indoor swimming pool and sauna, summer skiing on the Fee Glacier, a cinema with a variety of programmes each week, and several mechanical aids by which to reach high points above the village. One such, the Metro-

Alpin, is the world's highest subway. Reached by way of the Felskinn cableway, it burrows through the rocks walling the Fee Glacier to emerge at a revolving restaurant on the Mittelallalin; an assault on the mountain world. A Visitor's Card, obtainable for a modest fee from the tourist office, enables reductions on the cost of parking, swimming, concerts etc. It is recommended to all who plan to spend a few days of their holiday here.

Other Valley Bases:
North of Grund, **SAAS BALEN** has limited hotel accommodation. It boasts an attractive church with an onion-spire and, on the edge of the village, the valley's oldest chapel still offering regular worship. Above the village to the east rise the Fletschhorn and Lagginhorn.

Mountain Huts:
Four main SAC huts serve mountains above the Saastal. On the eastern side of the valley the twin **WEISSMIES HUTS** (2,726m) are easily accessible from Saas Grund by way of the Kreuzboden gondola lift, followed by a little under an hour's walking. Offering bed spaces for 110, and with a guardian in residence from the middle of June until the end of September, these huts are ideally placed for climbs on the Weissmies, Lagginhorn or Fletschhorn.

About an hour's walk short of the Zwischbergen Pass above the Almagellertal stands the latest and last of the SAC's huts, the **ALMAGELLER HUT** (2,894m). This now makes a much shorter approach for climbs on the Portjengrat and Weissmies from the south, as well as opening another area for walkers. It is also very useful for the crossing of the Zwischbergen Pass.

The **BRITANNIA HUT** (3,030m) has been long-established and was provided by funds raised by the ABMSAC (Association of British Members of the Swiss Alpine Club). It sits in a cleft between the Klein Allalin and the ridge of Hinter Allalin with glaciers on either side. With 113 places and a guardian in occupation from early March until the end of September, the Britannia Hut is extremely popular for glacier tours and climbs on the Allalinhorn, Rimpfischhorn, Strahlhorn etc. It is accessible from the Felskinn cableway by a marked glacier route, or by a fine high-level path from Plattjen.

High above Saas Fee, tucked in a dramatic position on the wall beneath the Lenzspitze, is the **MISCHABEL HUT** (3,329m), owned by the Akademischer Alpen Club of Zürich. It can sleep 120, has a guardian during the main season, and offers some exacting climbs on the various peaks of the Mischabel group. It is approached from Saas Fee by way of a very steep path in about 4 hours.

Unusual signpost in Saas Grund

Route 12:   **Saas Grund (1,559m)-Saas Fee (1,809m)**
             (via Kapellenweg)

Grade:	1
Distance:	3kms
Height gain:	250 metres
Time:	1 hour 15 mins

In several valleys included within this guide there are pathways that link a series of religious shrines illustrating the various stages of the Passion of Christ. None is more prominent than that which extends between the outskirts of Saas Grund and Saas Fee. This is an ancient pathway and along it are stationed 14 small stone shrines (the first built in 1687), and an opulently decorated Chapel of St. Mary of the High Steps at which a festival is held each year on 8th September.

From Grund cross the road bridge over the Saaser Vispa river (on the road to Saas Fee) and immediately bear left on a river-side footpath that soon leads beside one of the village's campsites. Just beyond this take the path (signposted) leading to the right, soon climbing up the hillside. It will take you past all the shrines and the final Chapel, with some good views back into the valley and others - more spectacular - to the ice-fields hanging above Saas Fee. At the top of the path you emerge beside Saas Fee Post Office where a Postbus may be taken back down to Grund.

Route 13:   **Saas Grund (1,559m)-Sengg (1,798m)-**
             Saas Fee (1,809m)

Grade:	2
Distance:	4kms
Height gain:	250 metres
Time:	1½ hours

A somewhat devious route between the two Saas villages, it is however an interesting one that is worth taking. It wanders through woodlands and along a stretch of pastureland with views across the valley to the Weissmies. The little hamlet of Sengg, about halfway along the walk, affords a striking contrast to the sophistication of Saas Fee.

From the centre of Grund take the road towards Saas Fee, and on crossing the river leave the road in favour of a footpath to the right. Immediately after, bear left on another footpath leading between gardens and up the slope towards woods. When the path forks at the edge of the woods bear right and follow uphill among the trees until you come onto the road at a hairpin bend. At this hairpin a few paces later another path, very narrow, heads away from the road to the right and climbs steeply up grass slopes to bring you to a track where you again turn right.

Walk along this track for about 800 metres, enjoying some lovely views across the valley, until you come to a junction with a second track heading sharply to the left. (Signposted to Saas Fee.) Follow this to the little hamlet of Sengg where a footpath goes between the buildings and on towards some thick woodlands. Continue along the path to Hotel Fletschhorn *(refreshments)*, and then join a track heading directly to Saas Fee.

**Route 14:   Saas Grund (1,559m)-Gspon (1,893m)
              (Gspon Höhenweg)**

Grade:	2		
Distance:	15 kms		
Height gain:	712 metres	**Height loss:**	378 metres
Time:	5 hours		

The *Gspon Höhenweg* is one of the classic Saastal walks. It leads high above the valley through larch woods, over pastures and beside clusters of alp huts on its ever-varied journey. The highest part of the route comes some way before Gspon, by a little hut at 2,271 metres, and thereafter the path either follows the mountainside's contours, or makes a gradual descent. It is clearly defined and waymarked throughout; a very pleasant walk which leads to an attractive little village in lovely surroundings.

About 100 metres down-valley from the centre of Saas Grund a signpost on the right of the road directs the path to Gspon. Passing beside houses and tennis courts and behind the Kreuzboden/Hohsaas gondola lift the footpath leads to Unter den Berg, now being submerged by Saas Grund's growth. Here a signpost announces the *Gspon Höhenweg* where the way climbs quite steeply among trees and leads beside a little chapel dedicated to St. Joseph (good views) near a junction of tracks. Continue ahead, soon passing alp huts and making steady progress on a rising traverse of the mountainside. Saas Balen is seen some distance below, streams are crossed, an avalanche protection wall is passed and you come to Heimischgarten (2,074m) a restaurant *(refreshments)* with fine views across the valley.

Zig-zags take the *Höhenweg* up to another junction of paths. Ours bears left with more zig-zags, and comes onto a broad track for about two hundred metres before leaving it to the right. Through sparse woods for a while, then across pastures with lovely views, along a shelf of hillside and then into a knuckle of valley to cross the Mattwaldbach stream. Having climbed away from this the path now reaches its high point at Färiga (2,271m).

Contouring the mountainside beside a *bisse* (irrigation channel), the path then deserts it on a descent among larch and pine, maintaining a steady course now all the way down to Gspon.

Gspon has hotel and matratzenlager accommodation, refreshments and small store. Take the gondola lift down to Stalden for the Postbus back to Saas Grund.

Route 15: **Kreuzboden (Chrizbode) (2,397m)-**
Weissmies Hut (2,726m)

Grade:	2
Distance:	1.5kms
Height gain:	329 metres
Time:	45 minutes

A short but strenuous walk, this takes a steep path from the gondola lift station at Kreuzboden up the moraines of former glaciers to reach the two Weissmies huts. Standing side by side on a lofty shelf, they command magnificent views to the Mischabel peaks and the gleaming ice-fields above Saas Fee to the south-west.

The Kreuzboden lift is found a short distance down-valley from the square in Saas Grund. There is a second stage to the cableway, leading from Kreuzboden to Hohsaas, but only the first section is required for this walk.

From the lift station at Kreuzboden *(refreshments nearby)* take the signposted path behind it, heading north-east up a steep cone of moraine, as far as the huts which may just be seen from the start of the walk.

Route 16: **Kreuzboden (Chrizbode) (2,397m)-Triftalp (2,072m)-**
Saas Grund (1,559m) (via Panoramaweg Hannig)

Grade:	2
Distance:	4.5kms

Triftalp, above Saas Grund - Switzerland's highest peak, the Dom, in the background

Height gain: 49 metres   Height loss: 838 metres
Time: 2½ hours

With magnificent views accompanying virtually every step of the way, the path to Triftalp from the *Hannig Panoramaweg* is extremely steep in places and requires concentration. In other words, don't get too carried away with the scenery unless you are stationary!

From the Kreuzboden lift station take the footpath heading west. There is a direction post bearing the Panoramaweg heading, and the path is waymarked with red-white paint splashes. It leads across a rough hillside and among boulders, then becomes a fine belvedere that emerges onto the promontory viewpoint of Hannig (2,446m) where there are two bench seats and the path divides.

Ignore the path heading right, but continue ahead on a narrow trail descending among boulders and shrubs. It grows steeper and zig-zags to lose height, passes between trees under the gondola lift and comes to a broad track. Follow this to the left, then bear right at a junction to reach soon after the tiny semi-deserted hamlet of Triftalp. This consists of a picturesque whitewashed chapel, a few houses and hay barns. (About 1 hour 20 mins from Kreuzboden.)

Continue beyond Triftalp on a clear path *(refreshments 2 minutes beyond the hamlet)* which heads down through larch woods and eventually reaches Saas Grund in the bed of the valley.

Route 17: Kreuzboden (Chrizbode) (2,397m)- Almagelleralp (2,194m)-Saas Almagell (1,673m)

Grade:	2
Distance:	10kms
Height loss:	724 metres
Time:	3½ hours

Höhenweg Almagelleralp, otherwise known as the *Höhenweg Kreuzboden*, is as its name suggests, a high route along the mountainside linking the cableway station with that delightful meadowland of Almagelleralp in the Almagellertal. It is a scenic walk, not too demanding, on a good path.

Bear left on leaving the gondola station along a broad path (it is signposted) that crosses a service track for the lift. Soon you come onto a broad scar of a track that leads round the shoulder of the Weissmies with splendid views across to Saas Fee's ice-fields. Losing height you will come to a junction of tracks, and from here the walking begins to improve. Continue ahead, thus ignoring the right-hand track, now gaining views towards the head of the Saastal and the Mattmark lake. About ten minutes after this junction leave the broad track in favour of an old mule trail heading south.

There follows a very pleasant section. There are alternative paths dropping into the valley, but ours continues along the mountainside, climbs for a while and then curves into the Almagellertal at 2,392 metres. The valley below and ahead looks lush and quite welcoming. Descending now you come to the Almagelleralp *(refreshments, accommodation)* and soft meadows. (About 2½ hours from Kreuzboden.)

A good clear path now leads down through the valley to Saas Almagell, reached in about one hour from the alp. Postbuses serve the village for a return to your base.

Other Walks from Kreuzboden:

The Kreuzboden lift area offers a good selection of walks along the mountainsides and down to the main valley. A useful leaflet *(Wanderkarte)* is published by the company that operates the gondola lift. It details, in German, fourteen different outings of varying lengths, and is recommended.

Route 18: **Saas Almagell (1,673m)-Almagelleralp (2,194m)-Zwischbergen Pass (3,268m)-Saas Almagell**

Grade:	**3**
Distance:	**16kms**
Height gain:	**1,595 metres** **Height loss:** **1,595 metres**
Time:	**8-8½ hours**

The Zwischbergen Pass gives access to the remote valley of the same name which flows down to the border country on the Italian side of the Simplon Pass. This route describes the approach to the pass, and it is a long and taxing day's outing. Although it is a demanding walk the countryside through which it travels is an enchanting landscape, wild and lonely, and there are magnificent extensive views from the pass to make all the effort worthwhile.

From the village square in Saas Almagell follow direction signs for the Almagellertal. Heading eastwards you are soon out of the village and climbing a zig-zag path among trees and beside a cascade. Coming into the initial opening of the valley the path eases and crosses to the north side of the Almagellerbach stream by way of a bridge. The clear path leads alongside the stream with fine views ahead to the amphitheatre of mountains (the Portjengrat) closing the valley in the east. About an hour and a half after leaving Saas Almagell you come to the mountain inn at Almagelleralp *(refreshments, matratzenlager)*.

A choice of routes are on offer from the hotel. They later combine for the final climb to the pass, so it does not really matter which of the paths you choose. That which sets out behind the hotel is steeper, though shorter. It climbs to the north at first, then traverses eastwards for a while before ascending in tight zig-zags to cross the Rottalbach by way of a bridge, then swings into the Wysstal, at the head of which is the pass.

The alternative route from the Almagelleralp inn continues up-valley, now above the stream, to gradually ascend the hillside in a long loop, cutting back to join the previously described path near the Rottalbach stream.

Entering the steep, green Wysstal the route is waymarked with paint splashes. Ahead the ridge looms rather dramatically and, under a scudding sky, appears a forbidding place. But the path continues to climb into the wild inner recesses of the hanging valley, and - about 2½ hours from Almagelleralp - brings you to the Almageller Hut

(2,894m, *refreshments*). From here another hour is required to gain the pass. It's a rough trail among the debris of the mountains, but on reaching the saddle of the pass the world opens out in splendour. Glorious views, extensive, majestic, memorable, are spread before you; the big peaks above Saas Fee and a world of snow and ice crowned in the south-west by Monte Rosa.

The return to the Saastal by the same path is a long and tiring one, but it enables new vistas to be appreciated on the way.

Route 19:	**Saas Almagell (1,673m)-Zwischbergen Pass (3,268m)-Gondo (855m)**

Grade:	3
Distance:	24kms
Height gain: 1,595 metres	**Height loss:** 2,413 metres
Time:	10½ hours

A long and taxing route, this crossing is of interest to long distance mountain walkers intent on making a traverse of the region. It may be shortened by a night spent in either the hotel at Almagelleralp, or in the SAC hut an hour below the pass.

Follow Route 18 as far as the Zwischbergen Pass and descend on the eastern side over a barren landscape to the left of the little glacier (paint flashes). Find a narrow path leading down beside a fan of streams dropping quite steeply to the bed of the valley (Zwischbergental). Once in the valley proper the path leads along the left bank of the stream, passing a number of alp hamlets and isolated hay barns until reaching a road at the hamlet of Bord (1,359m, *refreshments, accommodation*). Follow the narrow road down-valley for a further 1½ hours to reach Gondo *(refreshments, accommodation)*. From here Postbuses run over the Simplon to Brig.

Route 20:	**Saas Almagell (1,673m)-Antrona Pass (2,838m)-Antronapiana (908m)**

Grade:	3
Distance:	22kms
Height gain: 1,165 metres	**Height loss:** 1,930 metres
Time:	8 hours

As was outlined earlier in the introduction to the Saastal, the Antrona

Pass was an important crossing on the trading route between the Swiss Valais and Italy. Even today there are signs of the importance of this trail, for sections of the medieval paving are still visible. It is a grand walk, strenuous in places, but always interesting. The Italian frontier is met at the pass, and the descent on the south-eastern side is both steep and very rough. Those who would decline travelling as far as Antronapiana could turn back at the pass (4 hours up, approximately 2 hours 45 mins down) and still have a good day's exercise. But for those determined to cross into Italy, remember to take your passport with you!

Take the signposted path from the village square at Almagell to Furggstalden (1,893m, 45 mins, *refreshments*), or make use of the chair-lift to conserve energy. Furggstalden is reached through pleasant larch woods on a popular path, and the chalets of the little alp occupy a grassy shelf at the entrance to the Furggtälli. From here the path wanders through pastures, gradually gaining height as it enters the valley proper among trees and beneath ski tows.

Wandering through the lonely Furggtälli the path remains on the north side of the stream. There are one or two farms, green pastures, patchy woodlands and rock walls containing the valley. Eventually you come to scree, and beyond this the route becomes steeper and more rough underfoot. Here and there you may detect signs of ancient paving and picture in your mind the mule-trains of old that worked their way over the pass. Cairns and paint flashes guide the route, and about four hours after setting out, you come over the final slabs to reach the pass. It is a wild and lonely spot.

(An hour's easy scrambling up the ridge to the left will bring you onto the Latelhorn (3,198m)).

The descent into Italy takes you steeply down towards the Lago di Cingino (2,250m) which you pass to your left, clutched as it is in its rocky bowl. From the huddle of alp huts a little south of the lake, the path drops into the bed of the valley and works its way now north-eastwards. Passing numerous barns and chalets you come to two further lakes, the first of which is dammed and has a service road leading down to Antronapiana (avoid this road) and the second, Lago di Antrona (1,073m), was created by landslip in 1632.

The path remains on the left-hand side of the valley and just beyond Alp Ronco joins a road which takes you down to Antronapiana *(refreshments, accommodation)*.

Note: A road leads east from Antronapiana for 16kms to Villa-dossola, which is in turn some 7kms south of Domodossola. From this town a Postbus may be taken back to Switzerland over the Simplon

Pass and down to Brig. For the energetic and enterprising mountain walker, however, a return to the Saastal could be made from Antronapiana by taking a path northward to the dammed lake of Bacino dei Cavalli, then north-east to cross the Passo di Pontimia (2,378m) which gives access to the Zwischbergental (once more in Switzerland). From the bed of this valley simply bear left and reverse the route (19 above) over the Zwischbergen Pass back to Saas Almagell. Allow two days for this return.

Route 21:   Mattmark Dam (2,203m)-Innere Bodmen (2,238m)-Mattmark

Grade:	1
Distance:	8 kms
Height gain:	156 metres **Height loss:** 156 metres
Time:	2 hours

An easy stroll that, save for a short uphill section, follows a regular even course around the dammed Mattmark lake at the head of the Saastal. Some would advocate beginning in Saas Almagell, thus adding about 1½ hours to the walk, or 2½ hours if returning to Almagell at the end of the circuit. However, there is a Postbus service to the hotel just below the dam, and a large car park for those with their own transport, and as the valley path from Almagell to the dam is not particularly spectacular (though pleasant enough) this route is written simply as a lake circuit. As such it will appeal to those requiring a short and undemanding ramble.

From the hotel at the end of the road (with views to the snout of the Allalin Glacier) go up to the western end of the dam and follow the broad track heading south beside the lake, passing through two short tunnels. Views ahead are over a wild landscape dominated by the peaks containing the Italian/Swiss frontier with the dip of the Monte Moro Pass in the south-east.

Remain on the low track when an alternative offers itself and continue to the far end of the lake where you will see an alp hut (Innere Bodmen). On crossing a stream pouring from the valley draining the frontier peaks you come to a junction of paths. That which leads off to the right climbs to the Monte Moro Pass, but we remain on the lakeside trail and begin the northward journey. Soon after this the path starts to gain height and swings up the rough slopes to the right in long loops before crossing a semi-moorland area. Across this, it then begins the descent towards the lake with interesting views

64

to the snow peaks rising above the far side of the valley. At the dam end of the lake cross the causeway and descend onto the road.

Route 22: **Mattmark Dam (2,203m)-Monte Moro Pass (2,832m)-Macugnaga (Staffa) (1,307m)**

round walk to Pass & back to Dam.
17km ~ 11 miles

Grade:	**3**
Distance:	**12 kms**
Height gain: **629 metres**	**Height loss:** **1,525 metres**
Time:	**6 hours**

Another of the Saastal's ancient trading routes, the crossing of the Monte Moro Pass is one of the best known walks in the area. Its popularity is assured by the wonderful view of Monte Rosa's great east face (the so-called 'mirror' wall) that it has on the descent into Italy. For those who intend going all the way to Macugnaga, do not forget to carry your passport in the rucksack.

Follow Route 21 (above) as far as the southern end of the lake where the Monte Moro path cuts away to the right a few paces after having crossed the footbridge over a stream. The path is clearly defined and it leads up into a wild, rough, boulder-strewn landscape grazed by a few cattle and sheep. The way crosses several streams and gains height economically. After about 3 hours or so you will come onto the pass to enjoy the sudden dramatic opening of a new world, a new valley system, a new vista of Monte Rosa's majestic face. Macugnaga lies far below.

Just below the pass on the Italian side a cableway offers a short-cut down to the valley. There is also a CAI hut, Rifugio Città di Malnate *(refreshments)*, a short distance away. However, the descending path is clear enough, if steep, and it leads in full view of Monte Rosa down to the Valle Anzasca, reached after a long and tiring descent walk.

Route 23: **Saas Fee (1,809m)-Längfluh (2,870m)**

Grade:	**2**
Distance:	**5kms**
Height gain:	**1,061 metres**
Time:	**3½ hours**

Gazing up at the snow peaks walling the valley above Saas Fee, one is struck by the great curtain of glaciers hanging there. It is that, more than anything else, which gives the region its character. A dazzling, gleaming cascade of ice above meadows of green. But there is one prominent break in this curtain; a long tongue of rock and moraine, a strip of brown and grey amid a turmoil of snow and ice. This is the Längfluh. From it the walker has a grandstand view into the Fee Glacier's icefall on the northern side, and across the buckled surface of the glacier to the south. Below, sprawling in its pastures, lies Saas Fee.

There is a cableway in two stages from the village to the upper rock tongue of Längfluh, and an hotel there from which there are fine opportunities to catch a magical sunrise. It's a popular place, a handy starting point for various climbs on the neighbouring peaks without having to make the long haul up from Saas in the pre-dawn darkness. But for the walker who wishes to gain an insight into the mysterious world of glaciers, the approach up this steep wall of rock presents a splendid opportunity to do just that.

Leave Saas Fee by a broad trail heading south across the open meadows, and take one of several signposted paths to Gletscheralp (2,130m, 1 hour) on the lower part of the Längfluh divide, passing on the way a glacial lake trapped below moraine walls. From Gletscheralp you look onto the icefall to the right; a convulsion of séracs and crevasses.

The path continues to climb, but steeply now with the gondola lift swinging overhead to Spielboden. This is reached in about another hour from Gletscheralp. At Spielboden *(refreshments)* it is quite likely that you will see marmots, as there's a colony here that has become rather tame. The final stage of the walk maintains steep progress with the glaciers even closer than before.

To return to Saas Fee, either retrace the upward path or take the cableway down to the valley. Do not be tempted to wander onto the ice without proper equipment or the company of someone experienced in glacier travel.

Route 24: Saas Fee (1,809m)-Mischabel Hut (3,329m)

Grade:	3
Distance:	5kms
Height gain:	1,520 metres
Time:	4½ hours

The Mischabel Hut occupies a stunning position among the rocks of the Schwarzhorn which is part of the north-east arête of the Lenzspitze. High above the valley the views are superb, but it's a long and wearying walk to get here. The path is clear and well-marked, but it is certainly one of the steepest in all the Valais, with countless tight zig-zags to contend with. This is definitely not a walk to attempt on the first day of a holiday!

It begins in the village square by the church and goes along a street heading south-west (signpost) and soon comes into meadows where there are various ski lifts. A clear path now heads up the mountain-side, taking numerous zig-zags initially up to Schönegge (2,449m) at a junction of paths. Ours continues steeply uphill, gaining height among the rocks and with views growing more dramatic the higher you go. The path will invariably have others on it, for the hut is popular with climbers and its situation is so grand as to attract fit walkers intent on the experience of staying overnight there. On finally reaching it you will no doubt appreciate the guardian's bottled drinks and refreshments.

Route 25: **Saas Fee (Felskinn) (2,991m)-Britannia Hut (3,030m)-Plattjen (2,570m)-Saas Fee (1,809m)**

Grade:	2
Distance:	11kms
Height gain:	39 metres **Height loss:** 1,221 metres
Time:	4 hours

✓ see Route 26

By taking advantage of the various cableways strung above the village, a fine selection of outings become available to the general walker who might otherwise have been daunted by the distance or height to be gained in order to tackle them. This is one such, a short glacier crossing (on a marked track, no special equipment necessary) leading to a popular hut, followed by an exposed path which runs along the eastern slopes of the Mittaghorn high above the Saastal. This takes you to the gondola lift station at Plattjen where a ride down to Saas Fee is possible, or for the keen walker an interesting descent may be made through woodlands.

Before setting out, check conditions on the glacier either at the tourist office or at the cable-car station. Every effort is made to keep a path open across the Chessjen Glacier during the summer, but conditions may vary from day to day.

The valley station for the cable-car leading to Felskinn is found in the meadows at the southern edge of Saas Fee. Take a morning lift to make the most of the day. From the upper station, which is also the

Allalin Glacier, with Rimpfischhorn (4199m) left, and Allalinhorn (4027m) right - seen from above the Britannia Hut.

terminus for the Metro-Alpin, bear left to find the start of the marked path across the glacier. DO NOT STRAY FROM THE MARKED ROUTE. Although a pathway is clearly made, the glacier is still potentially dangerous. There may well be a few narrow crevasses to step across, or they may be bridged with snow and, at certain times of the day, water will probably be running over the surface of the ice, so be properly shod. The track, made by snowcat, leads through the obvious pass of Egginerjoch with the red-brown rock tower of Egginer (3,366m) rising above to the left, and the billowing ice-fields to the right that form the lower slopes of the Hinter Allalin. The walk to the hut takes about 40 minutes.

At the Britannia Hut *(refreshments)* a view opens onto the Hohlaub and Allalin Glaciers, but it is worth scrambling up the easy rocks of the Klein Allalin (3,069m, 10 mins) to the east of the hut where a superb panorama displays the Allalinhorn (4,027m), Rimpfischhorn (4,199m) and Strahlhorn (4,190m) rising to the south and south-west. Snow and ice-fields gleam in the sun, and the great glacier passes of the Adler and Allalin, which played such an integral part in the exploration of the region by the pioneers, (especially those of Curé Imseng whose statue adorns the village square in Saas Fee), are clearly seen.

Leave the hut and go down the lower part of the glacier to the north (traces of path in the snow) to join a clear path leading over a rocky terrain and along the eastern slopes of the Mittaghorn way above the valley. It is a good safe path, but a little exposed in places, and it takes you among a rough boulderscape with interesting views along the valley ahead to the distant peaks of the Bernese Oberland.

Eventually the path swings leftward to cross a shoulder of the Mittaghorn, and a wonderful view is displayed of the Mischabel peaks to the west. Over the col you come to the Plattjen lift *(refreshments)* for those who wish to terminate the walk here and take a gondola down to Saas Fee. Our walk continues down now quite steeply to reach another restaurant (Berghaus Plattjen, 2,411m) overlooking the snow peaks to the south. Take either of the path options from here, for they will both lead through the larch woods and arrive back in Saas Fee.

Route 26:   **Saas Fee (Plattjen) (2,570m)-Britannia Hut (3,030m)**

Grade:	2
Distance:	5kms
Height gain:	460 metres
Time:	2 hours

This walk reverses part of Route 25 (above) and is offered as a suggestion because it is quite simply a most enjoyable outing, and one that ought to be tackled by those who might otherwise shy away from attempting the full route previously described.

Take the Plattjen gondola lift from Saas Fee. It is a most scenic ride, with the glaciers and snow-fields and lofty neighbouring mountains seen in a new light. On leaving the upper station *(refreshments)* take the path leading uphill behind the lift building, to pass through a rocky saddle. From here the path swings to the right through a wild boulder-scape, then begins to taverse the eastern slopes of the Mittaghorn and Egginer. Far below lies Saas Almagell. On the far side of the valley stretches the Almagellertal, while ahead can be seen the milky blue waters of the Mattmark lake and the Monte Moro Pass along the frontier ridge. In places the path is rather narrow and exposed, but it is a safe route and it leads in about an hour to a short descent section with the Britannia Hut seen ahead as a dark shape at the head of a snow-field. This snow-field turns out to be the lower slopes of a minor glacier. There will invariably be a track leading up it to the saddle on which sits the hut *(refreshments)*.

Route 27: **Saas Fee (Plattjen) (2,570m)-Hannig (2,350m) (The Gemsweg)**

Grade:	2
Distance:	9kms
Height gain: 446 metres	**Height loss:** 666 metres
Time:	3½ hours

The Gemsweg (Chamois path) is one of my all-time favourite walks from Saas Fee. It's a true delight with consistently splendid views and plenty of variety along the path. It goes through regions of lush shrubbery, among larches and over moraine walls. It crosses glacial streams, wanders beside a glacial lake and below the ice-fields themselves. There are wild flowers in early summer, but in the latter part of the season the shrubs begin to take on their autumn textures and the Gemsweg glows with colour.

The walk could equally be taken in either direction, but I favour this clockwise loop in order to enjoy the superb views of the Mischabel peaks. Although it only requires about 3½ hours of walking, it is the sort of outing that is worth making into a full day. Take a packed

The Britannia Hut (3030m), Täschhorn and Dom in the background

lunch for a picnic. There is also the opportunity to buy refreshments about halfway along the route.

Take the gondola lift from Saas Fee to Plattjen *(refreshments)* and from there descend on a path signposted to Berghaus Plattjen *(refreshments)*, and beyond this to a lower ski-tow/chair-lift. A Gemsweg signpost now directs the route straight ahead (westward) on an almost level path with views growing ahead to the Dom and its lofty neighbours. Continuing, the path leads among larches and shrubs, descending now and then round the mountainside, across streams issuing from the glaciers whose séracs are seen above, and you come to Café Gletschergrotto *(refreshments)*.

The path continues beyond, and comes close to the snout of the Fee Glacier with views up to the frozen cascades hanging from the Täschhorn. The Gemsweg winds among boulders and passes the north-eastern end of a barren plain of glacial debris within which is seen a little tarn. From here the way leads up a moraine bank, then steadily gains height along the slopes of the Mischabelhörner, crosses a stream or two and works its way towards the upper station of the Hannig gondola lift *(refreshments)*.

The panorama from Hannig is renowned. From the restaurant terrace a glorious vista of the snow and ice-gemmed cirque of mountains embracing the pastures of Saas, reveals itself in all its majesty.

Either descend to Saas Fee by cableway, or take the pleasant, easy track signposted from Hannig as the Waldweg, which leads down among the forests to the village. (About 1½ hours extra - recommended.)

Route 28: Saas Fee (1,809m)-Hannig (2,350m)-Mällig (2,700m)

Grade:	2
Distance:	4.5kms
Height gain:	891 metres
Time:	2½ hours

This walk exploits the magnificent panorama of snow and ice-capped peaks of Saas Fee that are to be had from the high mountain slopes to the north-west of the resort. From the belvedere of Mällig (Mellig) there is a memorable array of summits and valleys laid out for inspection. There are wild flowers on the approach, and possibilities of catching sight of marmots and chamois.

The start to the path is located near the Hannig gondola lift station in Saas Fee. It is signposted and leads clearly up the slope before veering right to pass through the neighbouring hamlet of Hohnegg (1,950m, *refreshments*). Among the woods this clear path works its way in long loops up towards Hannig. Signposts reassure at the junctions of other tracks, and you eventually emerge from the shade onto the grassy terrace of Hannig Alp below the upper lift station *(refreshments)*. There are wonderful views from here.

Behind the lift station another signpost directs the route uphill in zig-zags towards Mällig, a series of rocky mounds. From the top there are even more extensive views than from Hannig, making a lovely site for a picnic. Below, and to the north, runs a stone wall known as the *Chinesische Mauer;* the Chinese Wall.

Route 29: Grächen (1,618m)-Saas Fee (1,809m) (Höhenweg Balfrin)

Grade:	2-3
Distance:	19kms
Height gain: 752 metres	Height loss: 561 metres
Time:	6½ hours

There are many very fine long walks to be had in the Valais region, and the Balfrin High Route is one of the most well-known. It was opened as long ago as 1954 after substantial engineering works - that included tunnelling - linked a series of ancient shepherd's paths into a continuous route leading almost the length of the Saastal. It begins in the village of Grächen that actually occupies a sunny position above the Mattertal, a little south of the junction of that valley with the Saastal.

It's a long walk, but a delightful one that will occupy a good day's exercise. There are many ups and downs to contend with; the highest point being at Stock (2,370m), reached a little over two hours from the start. After Hannigalp (1 hour 20 mins above Grächen) there are no further opportunities for refreshments, so take a packed lunch and plenty of liquids with you.

There is a Postbus that leaves Saas Fee for Grächen first thing in the morning in summer (check times at the PTT, and arrange to buy your ticket in advance). An alternative is to travel to Grächen the day before and spend the night there in advance of the walk. The village has a varied supply of hotel and gasthof accommodation, and a campsite.

The walk begins in the centre of the village, soon passes a small tarn and follows broad ski tracks through the forest as far as Hannigalp

73

(2,121m, *refreshments*) with its huge views. Many High Route walkers avoid this initial 500-metre ascent by taking the Hannigbahn cableway, thus saving about 1 hour 20 minutes. A little below the restaurant the continuing path (signposted) heads east across the pastures, enters woods and then veers to the south round the spur of mountain high above the Saastal. Gradually gaining height, but dropping here and there to cross small ravines, the clear path brings you to the high point of Stock, cut from the steep rocky slopes of the mountain.

The *Höhenweg* continues its spectacular route high above the valley. It climbs and descends on a constant switchback. It cuts into rocky cirques, crosses wild streams, rough boulders and scree, and always enjoys those splendid views of the Saas mountains, or off to the north towards the Oberland peaks. On occasion the path becomes a little thin and exposed. Sometimes it almost disappears across a boulder-scape, but paint flashes direct the route on towards Saas Fee.

With the bridge crossing of the Biderbach stream Saas Grund is seen below in the valley, and one senses the journey is nearing completion - but there is still a fair way to go. The path begins to lose height gradually, crossing an area of alpenroses and pine, and eventually comes to the wooded outskirts of Saas Fee.

Other Routes from Saas Fee:

There's no shortage of outings from Saas Fee. All round the pasture bowl beyond the village are numerous footpaths that could be linked to make easy strolls suitable for families with young children, all in an idyllic setting. The Tourist Office publishes an excursion map *(Wanderkarte)* with many footpaths clearly marked in red, and with brief descriptions (in three languages) printed on the reverse.

There are those that go down to the Saastal, to Saas Grund or to Almagell, and these make for pleasant short strolls, or as preludes to longer walks already suggested. Study the map, or any of the footpath signposts that appear throughout the valley.

For the experienced mountain walker, equipped and knowledgeable as to the crossing of glaciers, the high country beyond the Allalinhorn ridge is a true wonderland to be explored. There are the great glaciers passes of the **Alphubeljoch, Allalinpass** and **Adlerpass** that enable some of the most spectacular Alpine scenery of all to be discovered. There are routes over to Zermatt, or Täsch. There are modest high peaks to be climbed; Allalinhorn, Alphubel, Rimpfischhorn and Strahlhorn. Modest peaks, perhaps, but giving a day's exercise amid the dazzling glory of the inner sanctum of this mountain world.

MATTERTAL

Position:	**South of the Rhône Valley and immediately west of the Saastal.**
Map:	**L.S. 5006 'Matterhorn-Mischabel' 1:50,000**
Bases:	**Randa (1,408m) Täsch (1,450m) Zermatt (1,606m)**
Tourist Information:	**Verkehrsbüro, 3921 Randa (Tel: 028 67 1677) Verkehrsbüro, 3921 Täsch (Tel: 028 67 1689) Verkehrsbüro, 3920 Zermatt (Tel: 028 67 1031)**

By virtue of the Matterhorn rising at its head, the Mattertal must surely be one of the most visited valleys in all the Alps. Throughout the year crowded trains drag themselves through this narrow, steep-walled trench bound for Switzerland's El Dorado. Throughout the year cars and coaches stream along the valley from Visp to discharge their passengers in the huge car park at Täsch for the final 6 kilometre-leg of the journey which must be made by local train to Zermatt.

Zermatt is very much a place of pilgrimage. Everyone wants to go there; mountaineers, walkers, skiers, tourists of every persuasion. Everyone has heard of the Matterhorn, everyone knows its unmistakable profile. Everyone wants to see it for themselves. And why not? It is, after all, one of the most beautiful mountains in the world, and one that everyone can view in comfort without the necessity of walking for several hours through wild terrain with a rucksack on the back. You can sit for hours at a restaurant in the sun, a cold drink before you, and gaze at a magnificent spectacle that is no less dramatic when seen from the valley that it is close to.

But there is more to Zermatt that the Matthorn - though that would be sufficient in itself to ensure a continuing popularity. Above this teeming resort will be found the greatest collection of 4,000 metre peaks in all of Switzerland. The Matterhorn is not even one of the loftiest, but one of a crowd - although it stands alone, aloof, apart from its neighbours. Many of these are not just big mountains, they are peaks of character, of substance, or great charm. There's Monte Rosa, for example, a great iced gateau of a mountain containing many individual summits above a tumble of glaciers, and Lyskamm as its close neighbour, ice-strewn and snow-billowed. There's Dent d'Herens, shy in the Matterhorn's shadow, daubed with glacial plaster. There's the wedge of Dent Blanche to the west, as grand from this view as it is from Bricola. There's the Ober Gabelhorn like a fang guarding the stiletto point of the Zinalrothorn, with the pyramid of the Weisshorn rising to the north along a great jagged wall. And there are so many more; snow peaks, rock peaks, broad domes of ice giving birth to a world of glacial splendour. A world with enormous appeal for mountaineers, a world no less appealing to the mountain walker. Zermatt has it made.

Yet grand as it may be, Zermatt is but one end of the valley, and there are other places in the Mattertal that also deserve to be visited. Randa squats wedged between the Weisshorn to the west and the Dom to the east. A straggling community of dark timbered barns and chalets, it has not yet been sandwiched by a rash of modern developments, although it is growing steadily. On its edge, beyond the pastures and small garden plots woodlands clothe the lower slopes of the mountains, and on the outskirts streams dash down from barely-perceived valleys containing ice-fields at their head and rocky peaks crowding above. There are valley walks and steep paths clambering up the hillsides to explore tiny alp hamlets off the route of the general tourist.

Täsch, too, has some fine country on its doorstep, and the walker will not be disappointed by one or two outings taken from here. It is just a shame that the character of the village has become so swamped by the enormous car park that fills the valley meadows to the west of the road in order to save Zermatt from a similar fate.

The Mattertal road climbs out of Visp in the Rhône Valley to share the same initial approach as that for the Saastal. But at Stalden where the valley forks, the Mattertal branches off to the south-west, climbing above a rocky gorge for something like ten kilometres, until St. Niklaus is reached. Although nowhere as large or important as Zermatt, St. Niklaus is however the main village in the valley, and one with a fine cross-country trail leading westward over the mountain wall by way of the Augstbordpass (2,894m) to Meiden in the Turtmanntal.

Beyond St. Niklaus the valley veers to the south and the road crosses to the right bank (east side) of the river, then goes through the village of Herbriggen, by-passes both Breitmatten and Randa, and then the pastures open out for the final run to Täsch with the gleaming snows of the Zermatt Breithorn dazzling at the head of the valley.

Main Valley Bases:

RANDA (1,408m) offers a quiet, low-key alternative to Zermatt. It's far enough away not to be subjected to the same pressures as its more illustrious neighbour up-valley, and retains the atmosphere of an alpine village more concerned with crops and cattle than with the demands of an international tourist trade. It has one or two hotels, a few apartments for rent and, on the southern outskirts of the village, a campsite with very good facilities and views up to the Rothorn. The village has only limited shopping facilities and tourist information. It is served by train on the Visp-Zermatt line.

TÄSCH (1,450) lies 4 kilometres to the south of Randa, and is the roadhead for all tourist vehicles in the Mattertal. (Permit holders only may continue on the road as far as Zermatt where they must park their vehicles before entering the resort.) Much of Täsch is given over to the Zermatt tourist traffic; a vast car park, an extremely busy railway station and souvenir shops between the two. There is a campsite beside the railway, and several 3-star hotels in the village. Shops, banks and tourist information office.

ZERMATT (1,606m) is one of the great resorts of the Alps, and one of those privileged few to have whole books devoted to them. Likewise the Matterhorn whose history is inextricably bound with that of Zermatt, for it was from here that the young Edward Whymper and his party set out on that summer's day in 1865 to make the first ascent of the mountain by the Hornli Ridge. Having successfully reached the summit on 14th July, Whymper and his six companions began the descent, but the relatively inexperienced Douglas Hadow slipped, pulling others with him, and had the rope not broken the whole party may well have perished. As it was, four men fell to their deaths and the news of the tragedy swept across Europe, thereby gaining the Matterhorn and Zermatt considerable publicity. Anything added here may seem superfluous; the amount of words written on the tragedy would overtop the Matterhorn itself. Both Zermatt and the Matterhorn are, quite simply, incomparable.

For those who require such things, the boutiques that line Zermatt's streets are filled with extravagant gifts, jewellery, fashionable clothes etc. that appear to have absolutely nothing to do with the life of a mountain village. However, it does also have its mountain equipment shops, its guides' bureau, its food stores. There are hotels of every degree of comfort, and matratzenlagers for the mountain

The busy main street of Zermatt

wanderer who does not mind the simple life. There is a Youth Hostel here, and a campsite on the northern edge of the resort. And, of course, plenty of climbers' huts high on the mountains. Every conceivable tourist facility has been provided; swimming pools, tennis courts, museum, cinema - and several cableways to whisk you away from the resort and up to the high mountainsides. The tourist information office a few paces from the railway station is worth an early visit. There you can get details of available accommodation, and purchase special walking maps of the area which will give plenty of additional ideas for rambles over and above those detailed below. No-one need ever run short of walking excursions from Zermatt, or of ideas to fill one's holiday. The main problem is coping with the crowds.

Mountain Huts:

A number of SAC huts, private inns and small hotels are situated high in the mountains bordering the Mattertal and giving access to climbs on all the main peaks, or providing an interesting destination for a day's walk. Among these huts are the following: The **HÖRNLI HUT** (3,260m) situated at the foot of the normal route up the Swiss ridge of the Matterhorn. As such it is always busy. It has accommodation for 50 and a guardian throughout the main summer season (mid-June to late September). Next door to it is the well-known **BELVEDERE HOTEL**, owned by the Zermatt commune and with approximately double the sleeping capacity of its neighbour. Accommodation in dormitories and bedrooms. A full meals service is provided, and there's a busy terrace restaurant with views across the glaciers to Monte Rosa.

The **SCHWARZSEE HOTEL** (2,583m), with a convenient cableway nearby, claims to be the most frequented hotel in the district. It has a wonderful position overlooking the valley, the great snow-bowl of Monte Rosa leading round to the Matterhorn, and across to the Ober Gabelhorn and its neighbours. The range of accommodation on offer covers varying standards of comfort. There is a terrace restaurant for day visitors.

The **SCHÖNBIEL HUT** (2,694m) makes a popular excursion for mountain walkers. It is set at a junction of glaciers, about 4 hours or so from Zermatt. Accommodation for 80 in its dormitories, and with a guardian in residence from April until the middle of September when meals are available. From here climbs are made on the Dent Blanche, Dent d'Herens, Pointe de Zinal, Matterhorn (Zmutt ridge) etc.

High above the Trift gorge, and at the base of the south-east ridge of the Zinalrothorn, the **ROTHORN HUT** (3,198m) is reached by a long approach of about 5 hours from Zermatt. It can sleep 100 and has a guardian from the end of June until the middle of September. Base for climbs on the Zinalrothorn, Wellenkuppe, Ober Gabelhorn etc. Two hours or so below this hut stands the refurbished **TRIFT HOTEL** (2,337m), a simple gasthof which has matratzenlager as well as bedroom accommodation.

The small and somewhat primitive **WEISSHORN HUT** (2,932m) is not recommended as an overnight lodging for walkers. With places for only 36 people, it is primarily the province of climbers tackling the Weisshorn, or making the arduous crossing of the Moming Pass. There is a guardian only at weekends and on public holidays in July and August. From Randa the approach takes about 4½ hours.

Also reached from Randa, but situated on the mountain wall to the east of the Mattertal, the **DOM HUT** (2,940m) is handy for mountaineers tackling climbs on the Mischabel peaks; Täschorn, Dom, Lenzspitze, Nadelhorn etc. It can accommodate 75 in its dormitories, and has a guardian in occupation during high summer (July and August) offering meals and drinks. About 4 hours from Randa.

About 3½-4 hours' walking from Täsch is the much-visited **TÄSCH HUT** (2,701m), base for climbs on the peaks that separate Zermatt's valley from that of Saas Fee, namely Alphubel, Allalinhorn and Rimpfischhorn. There's also the interesting glacier crossing of the Alphubeljoch to be made from here en route for Saas. The hut can sleep 60. There's a meals service from the middle of July until the end of August when a guardian is in residence.

The large **GORNERGRAT (KULM) HOTEL**, accessible by the famous railway, occupies one of the most notable sites in Switzerland, overlooking a fabulous skyline of snow, ice and rocky peaks stretching from Monte Rosa to the Matterhorn. Accommodation of various standards available and, of course, meals for day visitors as well as those staying overnight. A variety of descent routes to Zermatt, and a fairly straightforward crossing of the Gorner Glacier to the **MONTE ROSA HUT** (2,795m) are possible from here. The normal approach to the Monte Rosa Hut, however, is from the Rotenboden Station on the Gornergrat Railway. By this route, it is about 2 hours' walk. It's a large hut, with bed spaces for 128, and a guardian from the middle of March until mid-September.

There are other inns and hotels accessible from Zermatt, either by railway, footpath or cable-car. These include the hotel at **RIFFEL-BERG** (2,582m) on the Gornergrat Railway (also popular in winter) and the **GANDEGG INN** (3,029m) a little way above the Trockener Steg cable-car station (below the Klein Matterhorn). **FLUHALP**

The route above the Schalikin Gorge that leads to Schaliberg

(2,626m) has a tall timber-built hotel as popular with day-trippers as it is with walkers and mountaineers, with much to satisfy most tastes on the surrounding hillsides. At **TÄSCHALP** (2,214m) on the route to the Täsch Hut, there's a small inn set in good walking country.

Lodgings may also be found in several of the little hamlets scattered on the steep pastures above Zermatt.

Route 30:   Randa (1,408m)-Schaliberg (1,968m)-Randa

Grade:	2
Distance:	7kms
Height gain:	560 metres **Height loss:** 560 metres
Time:	3½ hours

On a green shoulder of hillside steeply above the Mattertal, with the Schalikin gorge immediately to the south and with the lovely peak of the Zinalrothorn above, there's the collection of alp huts of Schaliberg. They occupy a lovely spot; trees below, rocks above, and views across the valley to the Mischabel peaks. The huts are full of the romance of the sun-bright Valais, and on a summer's day Schaliberg is a peaceful place. But the walk up to it can seem rather severe in its steepness.

Leave Randa and walk up-valley beside the road until a few paces before reaching the entrance to the campsite, seen on the left. Cross the road and go over a bridge to the left bank of the river (west side) where you will find a footpath. Ignore this and walk straight ahead for about 60 metres to find a second, more narrow, footpath. Turn left and follow it among trees and shrubs until, after about 500 metres, you come to a farm. Immediately beyond the farm take another narrow path heading steeply uphill to your right. This leads along the northern edge of the Schalikin gorge with splendid views to its head where the Zinalrothorn stands above a tumble of glacier. The path takes you in tight zig-zags past several old hay barns. (Where alternative paths beckon, signposts point the way - usually to the north-west, always steeply.) At last you emerge onto the shelf of hillside at Schaliberg. (About 2½ hours.)

To return to the valley go down the same footpath until you reach the first junction. Here go left, descending to a rocky section protected by chains, then into the forest and soon following a line of 15 wayside shrines, the last of which is found a few paces from the river at another path junction. Bear left alongside the river. This path will take you back to a bridge leading to Randa.

Route 31: Täsch (1,450m)-Täschalp (2,214m)-Täsch Hut (2,701m)

Grade:	2
Distance:	9kms
Height gain:	1,251 metres
Time:	4 hours

The walk up to this hut makes for a pleasant outing. It leads through flower meadows, passes the collection of buildings of Täschalp, gazes onto some wild mountain scenery, and gives the possibility of catching sight of chamois. A road was made through the valley leading to Täschalp during construction of the Grand Dixence hydro-electric scheme (most of the southern valleys of the Valais region were in some way affected by this major project), and many visitors to this corner make part of the journey by taxi from the Mattertal. This route, however, is for walkers starting from Täsch railway station.

Walk up-valley a short distance along the village street in the direction of Zermatt, then turn left along another road bearing signs to Täschalp. Soon the road makes a left-hand bend. Leave it at this point and continue ahead between two hay barns along a track heading up the slope and into forest. The route becomes rather steep in places, leading deeper into the valley and crossing the road two or three times. After about 2 hours or so you will come to the flower meadows of Täschalp, with its inn *(refreshments)*, attractive little chapel and delightful views.

The road continues through the valley, but just beyond the inn bear left along a service track that climbs the mountainside towards the hut. Behind you to the north-west the Weisshorn grows in stature. Keep an eye out for chamois as you approach the hut. (This is reached in about 1¾ hours from Täschalp.)

The return to Täschalp will occupy about 2½-3 hours.

Route 32: **Zermatt (Sunnegga) (2,288m)-Ober Sattla (2,686m)-Täschalp (2,214m)**

Grade:	2		
Distance:	7kms		
Height gain:	398 metres	**Height loss:**	472 metres
Time:	2½ hours		

Ober Sattla is a grassy shelf of hillside high above the Mattertal that commands some lovely views to the Weisshorn and the Mischabel peaks. It's a popular picnic site from which it is an easy hour's descent to the Täschalp seen below. From Täschalp one may either continue to the Täsch Hut (see Route 31) or wander down-valley to catch a train back to Zermatt from Täsch itself. Or, of course, you could stay overnight at the Täschalp inn.

Take the 'Sunnegga Express' underground funicular from Zermatt to its hillside station on a shoulder of the Unterrothorn. From here there are various mechanical aids to higher points on the mountain; busy both summer and winter. Head north along a clear track to Tufteren (2,215m, *refreshments*, good views to the west) where there is a junction of paths. Continue straight ahead on an easy trail leading over pastures (the Tufteralp), gradually rising and becoming more narrow. At one point the route crosses a rough boulder slope with cables to aid the nervous. Beyond this section the path climbs steeply to gain the belvedere of Ober Sattla. The views from this point are splendid. Far ahead, beyond the Rhône Valley, can be seen the

Bietschhorn which stands above the Lötschental. To the east you will see the Täsch Hut; below lies Täschalp.

The descent route is straightforward. It winds steeply down to the meadows of Täschalp *(refreshments, accommodation)* in about an hour from the saddle. For the onward route to the Täsch Hut, see Route 31; to descend to Täsch, bear left and wander down the valley on the clear track.

Route 33: Zermatt (1,606m)-Findeln (2,051m)-Grüensee (2,310m)-Zermatt

Grade:	2		
Distance:	10kms		
Height gain:	704 metres	**Height loss:**	704 metres
Time:	3-3½ hours		

The hamlet of Findeln must be one of the most photogenic places in all of Switzerland; a steep slope of green meadow, a huddle of ancient hay barns and houses, a white-walled chapel - and beyond it, the Matterhorn. It's a hackneyed view, but who can resist it? It doesn't matter how many times you see it, it never fails to draw a gasp of pleasure. So this walk is designed around that view. It's a steep walk up from Zermatt, and although there are other, easier ways to get there by mechanical aid, one should earn the pleasure of this charming view!

Wander through Zermatt's main street towards the Matterhorn. On the southern outskirts of the village cross a bridge over the river to Winkelmatten (signpost to Findeln in 1¼ hours). Follow a broad track past some chalets with good views of the Matterhorn to the right and the Mischabel group to the left, then drop downhill to cross the dashing Findeln stream. Across this bear left and take a footpath climbing through pine woods, over the Gornergrat railway line, and continue up the south side of the Findeln gorge.

Coming out of the shadow of the forest the path divides. Bear left, cross the stream and ahead stands Findeln *(refreshments)*. Walk through the hamlet heading to the right in order to catch the classic postcard view, and continue up the slope towards Eggen *(refreshments)*. At a junction of tracks break away to the right on a downward sloping path. Pass a small tarn (Mosjisee), and soon after the path swings to the right to climb in long loops up the hillside among larches and shrubs with lovely views to the Ober Gabelhorn, Zinalrothorn and Weisshorn to the north-west, and the Matterhorn straight ahead.

Grüensee, with Zinalrothorn and Weisshorn

On coming to the Findeln Glacier Hotel (2,296m, *refreshments, accommodation*) bear left and, in a few minutes, you will reach Grüensee *(refreshment kiosk)*. This little tarn is often crowded on bright summer days with picnicking families around its edge. From it there are fine views to the big peaks walling the unseen Mattertal to the north-west. Above the tarn will be seen the gaunt moraines of the Findeln Glacier.

Return to the hotel where a choice of paths will take you back to Zermatt. Signposts conveniently point you in the right direction at path junctions.

Route 34: **Zermatt (Sunnegga) (2,288m)-Fluhalp (2,607m)-Findeln (2,051m)-Zermatt (1,606m)**

Grade:	1-2
Distance:	10kms
Height gain:	319 metres **Height loss:** 1,001 metres
Time:	2½-3 hours

Fluhalp makes a popular excursion from Sunnegga, an easy stroll along a broad path with lovely views. There is a lofty hotel from which numerous outings are possible for both walker and climber. Above it rises the Rimpfischhorn. Nearby flows the Findeln Glacier. Mountaineers with glacier experience can make the crossing of the Adler Pass to the Britannia Hut (see Saastal section) from the Fluhalp Hotel, while tourists should wander a little beyond the hotel to find a pair of small tarns below the glacial moraine. The return to Zermatt via Findeln is in full view of the Matterhorn.

Take the underground funicular to Sunnegga ('Sunnegga Express') and follow the broad path signposted to Fluhalp. It gradually gains height towards the east, with the Blauherd cliffs above to the left. A green shelf of hillside leads to Stellisee, a tarn busy with sunbathers and picnicking families. The path continues beyond the lake and brings you directly to the Hotel Fluhalp (about 1½ hours from Sunnegga; *refreshments, accommodation*). This high, wooden building is an extremely busy place, not only with day visitors, but with those seeking overnight lodging in a dramatic setting, and as a base for the many walks and climbs nearby.

For the route to Findeln there is a choice of paths to take westwards. Follow signposts towards Grindjsee (tucked in a deep fold of mountain and moraine), and on to Eggen (2,177m, *refreshments*) with magnificent views of the Matterhorn, and down to Findeln itself *(refreshments)*. Again, a choice of paths, all quite steep, will lead back to Zermatt.

Route 35: Zermatt (Sunnegga) (2,288m)-Stellisee (2,537m)-Oberrothorn (3,415m)

Grade:	2-3
Distance:	6kms
Height gain:	1,127 metres
Time:	4 hours

The Oberrothorn is not a difficult climb, but it does make a strenuous walk. From its summit one gazes over a remarkable panorama of snow, ice, rock and far below, green meadows. It's a useful acclimatisation route for those going on to higher things, or as a high point for energetic walkers whose ambitions do not stretch to the 4,000 metre summits spread around Zermatt's bowl like jewels on a tiara. By taking the 'Sunnegga Express' we save ourselves two hours of exertion at the start of the day, which is worth doing since a 4 hour ascent (plus rests) is quite sufficient for most mountain wanderers, especially as the descent will occupy a further three hours.

Follow Route 34 as far as the western end of the Stellisee tarn. There is a junction of paths. Head left (north) up the slope and, on being joined by a track from the left (Blauherd) wander eastward, steadily gaining height, to reach a large boulder at 2,751 metres. (Another junction.) Continuing, the track now swings to the north (left) and climbs to a saddle (Furggji, 2,981m). (About 1 hour 20 mins from Stellisee.)

To the left (15 minutes away) rises the Unterrothorn, to the right the Oberrothorn. Bear right on a narrow path leading up a rough slope. It is quite steep in places (some fixed ropes), with a likelihood of snow patches lying near the summit. Extra caution should be exercised when crossing these. From the saddle to the summit will occupy about 1 hour 15 minutes. (Allow 3 hours for the descent to Sunnegga.)

Route 36:	**Zermatt (Gornergrat) (3,090m)-Riffelberg (2,582m)-Zermatt (1,606m)**

Grade:	**1-2**	? possible walk along path above
Distance:	**10kms**	Gorner Glacier
Height loss:	**1,484 metres**	
Time:	**3½ hours**	

Of all the tourist excursions available from Zermatt, a ride on the Gornergrat railway to see the renowned panorama overlooking the mass of glaciers pouring from Monte Rosa must, surely, rank as one of the most popular. The view is familiar from calendars, chocolate boxes and numerous books; sometimes claimed to be the finest accessible viewpoint in all the Alps. To walk there and back from Zermatt would make a long day for most ramblers, but to ride up by train and then walk down by any one of a variety of routes, is to create an entertaining outing. There will always be plenty to look at.

Choose a clear, fine day and take a morning train to Gornergrat - the earlier the better. The journey takes about 40 minutes, and as you gain height so the mountains grow more spectacular. (Choose a seat on the right-hand side of the carriage, facing the upward route, if you can.) The panorama displayed before you on arrival at Gornergrat is immense. The huge snowy block of Monte Rosa dominates everything, its glaciers hanging in motionless waves. Next to it rises Lyskamm, with the Breithorn, broader yet lower, standing beyond

Castor and Pollux, and the Matterhorn isolated in the west revealing a true pyramid shape. The Dent Blanche is the farthest big peak in the west, but on show too are the lovely Ober Gabelhorn, Zinalrothorn, Weisshorn, and the Mischabel summits to the north. Refreshments and accommodation are available at Gornergrat.

• The walk down begins on the south side of the railway and passes through a rather barren region of almost arctic tundra, but with staggering views, and with the great sweep of the Gorner Glacier below. On reaching the Riffelberg Hotel (2,582m, *refreshments*) a number of routes present themselves. Take the path down over meadows of poor grass, with a few steep zig-zags, to Riffelalp (2,222m) where there are two chapels; one Catholic, the other Protestant. Again, a choice of routes: either descend by the left-hand path through the forest to Blatten, and from there to Zermatt; take the middle trail directly to Zermatt via the Riffelalp Station, or choose the right-hand path which will lead to Findeln, then down to the valley. The choice is yours. Each is rewarding in its own way. Each will have sufficient direction markers along the way to guide you.

Route 37:   **Zermatt (Riffelalp Station) (2,211m)-**
                Riffelsee (2,757m)-Rotenboden (2,815m)

Grade:	2	*✓ ? could be combined with route 36*
Distance:	7kms	
Height gain:	546 metres	
Time:	2 hours	

The view of the Matterhorn standing on its head in the clear waters of the little Riffelsee is one that is regularly featured on postcards and calendars. This walk gives an opportunity to capture that view too.

Take the Gornergrat railway as far as Riffelalp Station, and from there walk up to Riffelalp itself to find the two chapels referred to in Route 36 above. From here follow the path heading south, marked to Gakihaupt (Gagihaupt), Rotenboden and Gornergletscher. It's a pleasant walk. You will cross a stream or two draining the slopes of the Riffelberg, and curve round the west face of it with the Matterhorn in full view, until the path begins to veer round to the south-east when new vistas open up. The path steadily gains height and reaches the rocky outcrop of Gakihaupt. (Another path junction.) Continue ahead through a narrow trough of a valley created between the slopes of the Riffelberg to the left and the ridge of the Riffelhorn to the right.

(The little rock peak of the Riffelhorn has some complex routes on its Gorner Glacier face; although short, there are a number of technically difficult test climbs which make it rather useful as a training ground. Non-climbing walkers are advised against being drawn to scrambling on it!)

Shortly after passing the peak of the Riffelhorn the path climbs up to reach the Riffelsee tarns. The view from the eastern shore of the larger lake will have you reaching for your camera and it is very tempting to spend a long time here on a warm day, simply enjoying the scene. Above to the left now is Rotenboden Station (a halt only). To reach it, continue along the path until you come to a junction. Here bear left and walk up the slope to reach the railway.

Route 38:   Zermatt (Riffelalp Station) (2,211m)-Riffelsee (2,757m)-Gorner Glacier-Monte Rosa Hut (2,795m)

Grade:	3
Distance:	12kms
Height gain:	584 metres
Time:	4½ hours

The route to the Monte Rosa Hut involves the crossing of the Gorner Glacier by a marked path. However, it is not a crossing that should be taken lightly for crevasses abound and precautions should be taken. Inexperienced walkers are advised against tackling it.

Follow directions for Route 37 above, until the junction of paths is reached a little beyond the Riffelsee. Instead of heading left as for Rotenboden Station, continue ahead on the clear path slanting down to the north bank of the glacier. On reaching the glacier follow the precise line marked. DO NOT STRAY FROM THE MARKED ROUTE. Tracks of previous walkers will undoubtedly be clearly visible. They will lead to a rocky outcrop marooned among converging cataracts of ice. Below this the path winds round to climb steeply a scree slope to gain the hut *(refreshments)*. (About 2½ hours from Riffelsee.)

The icy world revealed from the hut is indeed very grand. Especially fine are the glaciers bursting from the Lyskam, while the view of the Matterhorn is also notable.

Allow 2½ hours for the return to Rotenboden for the train back to Zermatt.

The hamlet of Zum See above Zermatt

Route 39:   Zermatt (1,606m)-Schwarzsee (2,552m)

Grade:	2	✓ *busy at top, near tarn.*
Distance:	7kms	
Height gain:	977 metres	**Height loss:** 31 metres
Time:	2½ hours	

Along a steep path through forest and open grassy slopes with the Matterhorn looming above, this walk is another of Zermatt's classics. For much of the way there will be few enough people on the path, but as you come onto the high shelf above the little lake, all the world seems to have arrived too. There is a cable-car ferrying tourists from Zermatt to the Schwarzsee Hotel, and the lake itself makes a honeypot of a picnic site, with its tiny whitewashed chapel being another of those easily recognisable landmarks of the region.

Wander south through Zermatt's streets, lured by the Matterhorn ahead. Follow signposts directing the path to Zum See first along the west bank of the Zmuttbach stream, then across it to the left on a bridge which leads to forested slopes. Zum See (1,766m, *refreshments*) is a pretty collection of hay barns and chalets and an attractive little church set in an undulating meadow. The path climbs above this

90

hamlet in steep zig-zags, passes an isolated house, Hermetji (2,053m, *refreshments*), and continues through forest until you emerge above the treeline to see the Matterhorn appearing rather foreshortened above.

In a little over two hours you will top a rise a few paces from the Schwarzsee Hotel (2,583m, *refreshments*) and there below, nestling in a deep bowl, is the lake. From it there are grand views to the Ober Gabelhorn.

Route 40:	Zermatt (Schwarzsee Hotel) (2,583m)- Hörnli Hut (3,260m)

Grade:	2
Distance:	5kms
Height gain:	677 metres
Time:	2 hours

The Hörnli Hut, with the large Belvedere Hotel next to it, is situated at the foot of the steep Hörnli ridge of the Matterhorn, by which the mountain was first climbed. This approach is extremely popular, not only with climbers, but with walkers who wish to get as close to the mountain as possible in order to experience some of its unique atmosphere. A popular walk it may be, but it is also a strenuous one and, it should be said, not particularly attractive in itself. The terrain is colourless, the nearby glaciers often dirty through the summer unless there's been recent snowfall, and the view of the Matterhorn is not as appealing as when viewed from a greater distance. It is tempting, though it may be heresy to admit it, to say that the closer one draws to the Matterhorn, the more it appears to be just a giant heap of rubble! Let those who climb it openly acknowledge that fact! However, where this walk scores is in the broader view; the side-long vision of Monte Rosa across the rivers of ice, the view north to the Dent Blanche, Ober Gabelhorn, Wellenkuppe, Zinalrothorn and Weisshorn, and off to the north-east where the Mischabel wall fades into shadow. From a little way above the hut there is a clear view onto the Matterhorn's north face - a forbidding place.

Either walk up from Zermatt as per Route 39 above (in which case it will mean a 4½-5 hour approach), or take the cable-car to the Schwarzsee Hotel. A clear broad path, signposted from the hotel, leads above and to the left of the lake. It is so well-defined and busy that detailed descriptions are unnecessary. It climbs, very steeply in places, the series of steps in the lower ridge. At first over grassy hillsides, then the terrain becomes more barren and rocky. In places

Schwarzsee, below the Matterhorn

the path has fallen away and a metal catwalk has been provided. There are a couple of sections where metal ladders ease the ascent of particularly steep crags, but mostly the walk is on a broad winding path, later over screes and last of all up a rocky spur with the Matterhorn looming steeply overhead. Distant views make the approach more interesting.

The Belvedere Hotel adjacent to the Hörnli Hut has a terrace restaurant overlooking the Furggletscher. From the terrace you may be able to see climbers on the ridge of the mountain above.

Route 41:   Zermatt (1,606m)-Zmutt (1,936m)

Grade:	1
Distance:	3kms
Height gain:	330 metres
Time:	50 minutes

A short easy walk on a broad path to a pretty hamlet, this takes care of a half day when perhaps you need to flee the crowds in the town, or you've got a train to catch home later in the day and need just one last stroll with a view. (Although that view will be somewhat restricted.) Zmutt sits among lovely flower meadows with a partial view up to the north face of the Matterhorn. It's a small place, a huddle of wooden hay barns and slate-roofed houses, a tiny chapel and a few restaurants.

Leave Zermatt on the track heading south towards the Matterhorn. Signposts at regular intervals keep you along the main path with the river to your left. The climb is a steady one leading through the woods and out to open meadows. A few minutes before reaching Zmutt you come to a farmhouse *(refreshments)*. Beyond it lies the little hamlet *(refreshments)*. Allow 40 minutes for the return to Zermatt.

Route 42:   Zermatt (1,606m)-Zmutt (1,936m) (via the high path)

Grade:	2
Distance:	3.5kms
Height gain:	414 metres
Time:	2 hours

This route to Zmutt is more appealing to walkers than the above alternative. It is certainly more strenuous, but the rewards are greater in the views.

Walk towards the Matterhorn through Zermatt's main street. Shortly after you pass the church the street bends and you will see a footpath signpost pointing along a side street on the right to Herbrigg, Hubel and Zmutt. The street takes you past a few houses, climbing steadily out of the village to a path, and then more steeply through hay meadows. Passing the hay barns of Herbrigg (30 minutes) and Hubel (1¼ hours) the path climbs again, then contours along a delightful

Ober Gabelhorn, Zinal Rothorn and Weisshorn, seen from the path to the Matterhorn's Hörnli Hut

grassy terrace with views up to the Matterhorn and over to the Mischabel chain. On coming to a path junction bear left to descend among rock bands to Zmutt. (The right-hand, or continuing, path goes to the Schönbiel Hut and joins the main route from Zmutt a little farther to the west.)

Route 43: **Zermatt (1,606m)-Schönbiel Hut (2,694m)**

Grade:	2-3	
Distance:	11kms	
Height gain:	1,088 metres	
Time:	4 hours	

22 kms

Took us 3½-4 hrs out. 3¼ hrs back.

Very strong wind dust on moraine

Many regard this walk as the very best of all Zermatt's outings. It is a scenic route, apart from the gaunt and unlovely surroundings of the hydro-electric scheme below the Zmutt Glacier, and the site of the Schönbiel Hut is a stunning one. As the approach is rather long, and

94

the return will require about three hours, make a point of leaving Zermatt early - unless you plan to spend the night at the hut. Note too, that there is little shade to be found beyond Zmutt, so on a bright summer's day it is a good idea to break the back of the walk before the sun has risen too high.

Follow Route 41 to Zmutt (1,936m, *refreshments*) and from there continue on a signposted path heading west along the valley, passing a dam that forms part of the complex Grande Dixence Hydro-electric system on your left. Beyond the dam the milky glacial water looks most uninviting, and the grey moraine deposits have a sorry appearance that will require the artistry of a vigorous vegetation to make good.

The views begin to open out as the path steadily gains height, and about an hour after leaving Zmutt you will reach the little restaurant of Kalbermatten (2,105m, *refreshments*) with its sudden view of the Matterhorn. Gaining height pass a trail that cuts away to the left, then climb a series of zig-zags beside a waterfall and come to another path junction. (This time the fork takes an alternative footpath off to the right, climbing round the Höhbalmen wall.) Ignore this alternative for we must continue ahead, over a footbridge, and soon cross the stony mouth of the Arben valley. Rising sharply at its head is the Ober Gabelhorn.

Beyond the Arben our path climbs onto the moraine wall and, growing more narrow, follows along its crest, finally slanting up in zig-zags to top the grassy slope on which sits the Schönbiel Hut *(refreshments)*.

The hut gazes across to the soaring form of the Matterhorn and its neighbour, Dent d'Herens. A sweep of ice comes pouring from north, south and west; frozen cataracts hang from mountain walls; crests of snow arch against the sky. The world dazzles in a confusion of splendour. Soak it all in and be thankful.

Route 44: Zermatt (1,606m)-Trift (2,337m)

Grade:	2
Distance:	3kms
Height gain:	731 metres
Time:	2 hours 15 minutes

Immediately to the west of Zermatt there's an absence of mechanical lifts, and as the mountains rise very steeply out of the valley, all but the most determined of mountain walkers seem to be deterred from exploring there. But in many ways the Trift region offers some of the finest walking of all from Zermatt. This outing leads through the Trift gorge, the key to some splendid country. It takes us to the simple mountain inn of the Trift Hotel, a renovated Victorian building with matratzenlager accommodation and individual bedrooms available.

Near the Monte Rosa Hotel in Zermatt's main street find a narrow lane with a signpost directing to Edelweiss, Trift etc. The lane winds up between chalets and hotels, and when it finishes a footpath continues across meadows towards the Trift gorge. A strengthened wooden bridge leads over the stream that comes dashing through the gorge, and the path then zig-zags among trees to gain the dramatic viewpoint of Alterhaupt (1,961m) where you will find the Edelweiss restaurant (about 1 hour; *refreshments*). This is a popular spot with visitors to Zermatt, for there is a splendid birds's-eye view of the town steeply below.

The footpath continues, descending a little, then levelling among trees before climbing steeply once more. After a while you cross back to the north side of the stream at a rocky step and climb on; a strenuous ascent of the gorge with the Ober Gabelhorn making a spire high above, and with the Wellenkuppe wearing a crown of snow next to it.

On reaching the head of the gorge you enter a broad grassy plateau with the Trift Hotel *(refreshments)* standing beside the path. Ahead rises a lovely cirque of mountains and glaciers; behind in the east gleams the Monte Rosa group; below yawns the gorge. It's a fine place for a picnic.

Route 45: Zermatt (1,606m)-Trift (2,337m)-Mettelhorn (3,406m)

Grade:	**3**
Distance:	**7kms**
Height gain:	**1,800 metres**
Time:	**6 hours**

The ascent of the Mettelhorn is justifiably included in this guidebook for walkers since it involves no technical difficulty or particular danger, and is rewarded by a summit panorama that has been applauded for well over a century. It's a long ascent. A long and strenuous day's outing with plenty of height to gain. Since the route passes the Trift Hotel door, it would be worth considering spending a night there prior to making the ascent, thereby saving at least two hours and 700 metres or so at the start of the day. One word of warning: do not tackle this if the preceding days have suffered bad weather, as subsequent snow conditions may well cause problems. An ice axe would be helpful. If starting from Zermatt, make certain to set out by 6.00 a.m. at the latest.

Follow Route 44 as far as the Trift Hotel *(refreshments)*. Continue along the path over the grassy meadows of the plateau and cross the stream near a waterfall. Ignore a turning to the right here where a path leads a little south of east and takes you back to Zermatt. Our path rises and comes to another junction of tracks (2,456m, 20 mins from Trift Hotel). Bearing left is the route to the Rothorn Hut (Route 46), but we take the right-hand option (signposted). The path climbs into the Triftkumme - a knuckle valley through which the route hauls itself. At first on grassy slopes beside a stream, then along a line of cairns through a rubble of rocks, heading north-east almost all the way. To the right the kumme is walled by a rocky crest that rises to the peak of the Platthorn. (The Mettelhorn is unseen from here.)

To the left of the Platthorn will be seen an obvious little saddle which has to be crossed. But first it seems that the cairns will lead to the Platthorn instead. As you draw closer the route wanders leftwards up a rocky area and over patches of snow to reach a permanent snowfield on the skyline. To the right will now be seen the Mettelhorn. Cross the snowfield and climb the final cone of loose stones to the summit.

As a just reward for the effort of getting here, the summit panorama is a prize to remember. It includes all the main peaks of the Zermatt area; Monte Rosa, Lyskamm, Breithorn, Matterhorn, Ober Gabelhorn, Zinalrothorn etc. The Weisshorn looms to the north-west. Across the valley stand the Mischabel peaks with the Dom and Täschhorn particularly domineering. Far beyond the Rhône Valley can be seen the snowpeaks of the Bernese Oberland.

Allow 4 hours for the return to Zermatt.

Route 46:   Zermatt (1,606m)-Trift (2,337m)-Rothorn Hut (3,198m)

Grade:	**3**
Distance:	**7kms**
Height gain:	**1,592 metres**
Time:	**5 hours**

Another stiff walk, but as with the ascent of the Mettelhorn, the views are worth the effort. The Rothorn Hut is base for climbs on such peaks as Zinalrothorn, Wellenkuppe, the twin Äschhorn summits, Trifthorn and Ober Gabelhorn. Set at the base of the south-eastern ridge of the Zinalrothorn, it has glaciers to left and right, and a great sweep of mountainside plunging steeply to Trift.

Follow Route 45 to the junction of paths at 2,456m, some twenty minutes above the Trift Hotel. Here bear left to head north-westwards up the scree-carpeted slopes with the steep rocky wall ahead sweeping round towards the Platthorn. Crossing a stream go up onto the crest of the moraine formed by the Trift Glacier. The ascent to the hut from here is direct and steep, and it is with some relief that you come onto the little promontory on which it is set. *(Refreshments)* Allow 3½ hours for the descent.

Route 47:	Zermatt (1,606m)-Trift (2,337m)-Höhbalmen (2,741m)-Zermatt

Grade:	2		
Distance:	18kms		
Height gain:	1,135 metres	Height loss:	1,135 metres
Time:	7 hours		

This long and strenuous walk round the Höhbalmen wall above Zmutt is one of the finest of all Zermatt's outings for the fit mountain wanderer. It is a scenic outing with extensive views of a great array of 4,000 metre peaks. Choose a clear fine day, make an early start and take your camera along.

Take Route 44 as far as the Trift Hotel (2 hours 15 mins, *refreshments*) and there you will find a footpath heading left (south) signposted to Höhbalmen. Cross the stream and wander over the hillside, steadily gaining height towards the south-east where, an hour or so after leaving Trift, you round the shoulder of mountain which forms the southern wall of the Trift valley, to be greeted by a view of the Matterhorn that will have you reaching for the camera. Continuing along a terrace, so the view extends to include many glorious mountains, snowfields and glaciers.

The path continues, now towards the south-west and later, way above the hamlet of Zmutt, heads westward to reach the high point of the walk, marked on the map as Schwarzläger. The path now begins to lose height as you come to the mouth of the Arben valley below the Ober Gabelhorn, and descends through pastures to join the Zermatt-Schönbiel trail (Route 43 above). Turn left and follow this path back to Zermatt (about 2 hours) via Zmutt *(refreshments)*.

Other Routes from Zermatt:

Those routes outlined above represent, perhaps, the very best of

Zermatt's outings for walkers. The list is by no means comprehensive though, and enterprising mountain walkers will gain plenty of enjoyment from working out additional routes suggested by the map of the region.

Based on the town there are countless short walks that would take care of half a day, or even a summer's evening. Signposts appear everywhere. It's almost impossible to get lost. There's the down-valley walk to **Täsch**, easy among woods and over meadows, or along to **Ried** through trees. The **Gorner gorge** is worth a visit for its water-falls; **Zum See** will reward too And by taking any of the cableways or mountain railways onto the hillsides there are gentle strolls to be had in a wonderland of high mountain scenery.

The Zermatt *Exkursionskarte*, available from the tourist office near the railway station, is a 1:50,000 scale L.S. map overprinted with walking routes, and is highly recommended.

In the past mountain huts were supplied by mule or porter. Nowadays helicopters are used.

Grimentz

VAL d'ANNIVIERS

Position:	**South of Sierre in the Rhône Valley.**
Map:	**L.S. 5006 'Matterhorn-Mischabel' 1:50,000**
Bases:	**Zinal (1,675m) Grimentz (1,572m)**
Tourist Information:	**Office du Tourisme, 3961 Zinal**
	(Tel: 027 65 1370)
	Office du Tourisme, 3961 Grimentz
	(Tel: 027 65 1493)

Val d'Anniviers is a magical place. As you enter from the broad vine-clad Rhône, swinging in tight hairpins to gain the height required in order to get onto the eastern shelf of the valley, there's a sense of grandeur about the long open tunnel stretching ahead. At first it's green and the hillsides dense with forest and shrub, the river below scouring a deep bed to ease access for future generations. A summer warmth buzzes from the lush vegetation, but a gleam of ice and snow at the head of the valley promises even better things, and as you draw closer, so that promise becomes a reality. Up there, at the very head of the valley, is some of the loveliest mountain scenery imaginable.

The Val d'Anniviers has often been hailed as the grandest or greatest of all the Swiss valleys of the Pennine Alps; and who would dispute it? Some sixteen kilometres or so from Sierre it divides into two distinct branches. The main branch continues slightly east of south as the Val de Zinal, while that to the south-west becomes the Val de Moiry. Both branches have great potential for the mountain walker and lover of fine scenery.

Heading then along the Val de Zinal one is drawn by the towering rock peak of Lo Besso (3,668m) whose domination of the valley is only lessened when Zinal itself has been left behind. When the road runs out south of Zinal and you take to the footpaths, Lo Besso is put into perspective, and it is then the great ice-caked peaks that show their worth: Weisshorn, Schalihorn, Pointe Sud de Moming, Zinalrothorn. A fabulous cirque of mountains blocks the southern end of the valley and swings round to the west of the deep glaciated trench: Ober Gabelhorn, Mont Durand, Pointe de Zinal, Dent Blanche,

BREITHORN · MATTERHORN · DENT · DENT BLANC · OBER GABELHORN · WEISSHORN · VAL DE MOIRY · ZINAL · GRIMENTZ

Grand Cornier, the airy ridge of the Bouquetins and Pigne de la Lé. Several of these peaks are over 4,000 metres high, the remainder pushing close to that elevated point. Glaciers hang suspended from walls of rock, one peak laced to another by waves of glistening cornice, while below the ice-sheets sweep together in an arctic crevasse-sliced river.

But while the snow and ice peaks hold one's attention, there are green shelves high above the valley with scattered alp huts here and there with narrow paths meandering between them. These paths give access to that special wonderland - the middle mountain kingdom. It is this region that affords some of the very best of all mountain views. It is from this region that the mountains begin to reveal their secrets.

They certainly do above the Val de Zinal. The alps of Combautanna and of d'Ar Pitetta on either side of Roc de la Vache on the eastern slopes, are the very substance of dreams, and almost opposite these, on the western hillside, La Lé is a green bowl of splendour with views to hold onto long after you return home.

Val de Moiry too leads into realms of enchantment. But here one must go deeper, for the dam at the northern end of the Lac de Moiry reservoir projects its concrete presence over part of the valley. However, south of the lake there is another icy world of great charm, with glaciers pouring from the heights in one of the most dramatic and turbulent icefalls to be seen anywhere in the Alps. The approach to the Moiry Hut gives a close view of this icefall, and a privileged introduction to the inner sanctuary of the high mountains.

Main Valley Bases:

ZINAL (1,675m) is a small village and long-time mountaineering centre that is being steadily developed to attract winter visitors too. At present the majority of buildings in the village are traditional Valaisian structures of dark timber; hay barns and chalets stand cheek-by-jowl above the river to the east. There are several hotels and pensions offering accommodation, some have dormitories available and there's a campsite to the south of the village. In Zinal there are two or three restaurants, a choice of shops, Post Office, mountain guides' bureau and tourist information office. There is an indoor public swimming pool, and there are tennis courts etc. One cableway swings visitors onto the high mountainside; this goes to Sorebois to the north-west of the village.

GRIMENTZ (1,572m) must rank as one of the most attractive villages in the Valais region. It is set at the mouth of the Val de Moiry on a steep slope of hillside, dark timbered chalets and barns standing in tiers one above another, their windows adorned with boxes of geraniums and petunias, their alleyways narrow and filled with shadow. As with Zinal, Grimentz is also growing in a bid to attract more winter visitors. There are several hotels; one, two and three-star rated. There are cafés and restaurants, a few shops, Post Office and tourist information. Heated indoor swimming and tennis courts etc. are provided for visitors.

Other Valley Bases:

There are several villages in the Val d'Anniviers, in addition to Zinal and Grimentz, which have varied amounts and standards of accommodation available. Set on a green terrace above the valley to the east is the high-lying village of **CHANDOLIN** which has two hotels and a

Wood carvings on a chalet wall in Zinal

number of apartments for rent. **ST. LUC, VISSOIE** and **AYER** each have campsites and a limited supply of hotel accommodation.

Postbuses serve both stems of the valley, and even go as far as the dam at Lac de Moiry.

Mountain Huts:

Working clockwise round the head of the Val d'Anniviers, those huts accessible from the valley begin with the **CABANE de TRACUIT** (3,256m) perched high on the col of the same name between Les Diablons and Tête de Milon. With 112 places and a guardian in residence from the middle of June to mid-September, it is reached by a steeply climbing path from Zinal in 4½-5 hours.

Below the west face of the Weisshorn in a glorious cirque of dazzling ice, the **CABANE d'AR PITETTA** (2,786m) gives access to the Crête de Milon and the Weisshorn. It is only a small hut with places for 20, and as there is no resident guardian meals are not available. Self-catering only. About four hours' walk from Zinal.

CABANE du MOUNTET (2,886m) occupies an enchanting position on the rocks that form the southern ankles of Lo Besso.

Facing the magnificent cirque of mountains that close the valley, the hut is in a privileged position for climbers tackling such peaks at Zinalrothorn, Trifthorn, Ober Gabelhorn, Mont Durand, Pointe de Zinal etc., as well as the easier Lo Besso itself. By way of the Glacier and Col Durand, the Schönbiel Hut above Zermatt may also be reached. Cabane du Mountet is reached in about 5 hours from Zinal, has a guardian in occupation from early July until mid-September, and can sleep 115 in its dormitories.

Below the Mountet Hut, and perched upon the moraine wall bordering the Zinal Glacier, is the privately owned **CABANE du PETIT MOUNTET** (2,142m). Reached by way of a good path from Zinal in a little under two hours, this hut offers dormitory accommodation (telephone in advance for reservations: 65 1380) and restaurant facilities. With lovely views and easy access it is a popular site for a picnic.

There is only one SAC hut in the Val de Moiry; **CABANE de MOIRY** (2,825m). This is in yet another idyllic site, overlooking as it does the stupendous icefall of the Moiry Glacier and a horseshoe of shapely peaks. Among those peaks attainable from here are Grand Cornier, Pigne de la Lé and Pointes de Moiry. By way of the snowy Col du Pigne experienced mountain walkers can cross over to the pastures of La Lé and the Petit Mountet. Cabane de Moiry can accommodate 92 people, is reached in less than 2½ hours from the Moiry barrage, and has a guardian from July to September.

Route 48:   St. Luc (1,655m)-Hotel Weisshorn (2,337m)-Zinal (1,675m)

Grade:	**2**
Distance:	**16kms**
Height gain:	**765 metres** **Height loss: 745 metres**
Time:	**5½-6 hours**

Not a walk to attempt on the first day of a holiday, it is however a good introduction to the Val d'Anniviers, for it follows a high path over pastures and through larch and pine woods heading towards the magnetic ice-clad peaks that block the valley to the south. St. Luc, where the walk begins, occupies a sun-trap of a hillside way above the valley floor, and is reached by way of a hairpin road. The village is served by Postbus from Sierre or Zinal (change at Vissoie).

From St. Luc follow signs towards Hotel Weisshorn (later there'll be the letters H.W. painted on rocks to guide you, and sometimes the letter Z, indicating Zinal). The path heads eastwards, passes a chair-lift and soon begins to climb up the hillside through the *Forêt de Lache* to reach the big white building of Hotel Weisshorn (2 hours 15 mins, *refreshments, accommodation*) with its fine views over and along the valley.

Continue behind the inn as far as a junction of tracks where you will see a signpost directing the path to take towards Zinal. At first heading a little south-west, the path then veers more to the south to traverse below the ridge marked on the map as Pointes de Nava. Views to the head of the valley grow in stature as you wander along this stretch, and about three hours after leaving St. Luc you will reach the highest point along the walk at 2,420 metres. Signs keep you along the correct path where alternatives occur as you round the spur of Montagne de Nava. Cross two or three streams, bear round the Crête de Barneuza and gradually lose height down the hillside. At Alp Lirec (2,172m) the descent begins in earnest, dropping in a series of tight zig-zags to the valley floor at Zinal.

Route 49:	St. Luc (1,655m)-Bella Tola (3,025m)

Grade:	2-3
Distance:	6kms
Height gain:	1,370 metres
Time:	4½ hours
Additional map:	L.S. 273 'Montana'

This strenuous walk follows a good path all the way from St. Luc to the summit of Bella Tola where a marvellous panorama of peaks is laid out for inspection. This panorama includes Oberland peaks to the north, as well as the gleaming giants of the Pennine Alps to the south, east and west.

Leaving St. Luc follow signs to the Pierre des Sauvages, a large rock with inscriptions carved in it, long thought to be a Druidic altar stone. The way passes under the chair-lift that goes to Tignousa and, 1 hour 40 minutes after leaving the village, comes to Chalet Blanc (2,179m).

From Chalet Blanc either take the broad track north-westwards to the upper Tignousa chair-lift, and from there to the summit via Cabane de Bella Tola (2,346m, *refreshments, accommodation*); or head up the slope above the farmhouse on a path to Montagne de Roua (2,404m), and continuing, join the alternative trail up to the ridge running between the Rothorn and Bella Tola. Our summit is to the right, and the route to it, although a little exposed, should be safe and subject to no real difficulties. (Allow 3 hours for the descent.)

Routes between Val d'Anniviers and the Turtmanntal:
There are three passes which should be practical for walkers planning to cross the long ridge separating the Val d'Anniviers from the Turtmanntal (the divide between French and German speaking Valais). Each one may be attempted from St. Luc, and each arrives in the little village of Gruben (1,822m; *accommodation, refreshments, food store*).

The northern crossing is by way of the **PAS de BOEUF**; a route that could be linked with the ascent of Bella Tola, but markings are poor and in less than good visibility problems could occur.

The second crossing is by way of the well-marked **MEIDPASS** (2,790m), reached by way of Chalet Blanc (see Route 49 above) and the Lac de l'Armina. Signposts and the letters M.P. painted on rocks indicate the way. From St. Luc to Gruben will take about 6 hours.

FORCLETTA (2,874m) is the southerly of the three crossings and, from St. Luc, the longest. It is, perhaps, better suited for those leaving the Val de Zinal at the village of Ayer (1,476m). The route is waymarked via Tsahélette (2,523m) and will take between 5½-6 hours, Ayer to Gruben.

Cabane du Petit Mountet (2142m)

Route 50: **Zinal (1,675m)-Petit Mountet (2,142m)**

Grade:	**1-2**
Distance:	**5kms**
Height gain:	**467 metres**
Time:	**1 hour 45 mins**

This short and easy stroll makes an ideal introduction to the country south of Zinal. It gives a close-up view of the high peaks, their hanging glaciers and snow basins. There are, in fact, two routes. One, suitable for families, follows a broad and well-graded track for most of the way, while the alternative branches away from the track ¾ hour from Petit Mountet and climbs among shrubs on a narrow path that is rather steep in places. The Cabane du Petit Mountet is perched on the moraine wall bordering the Zinal Glacier, with a magnificent collection of high peaks in full view.

Wander up-valley from Zinal following the road along the east (right) bank of the river. When the road ends continue ahead along a vague track until you reach a wooden bridge spanning the river. Cross over and wind uphill on a clear broad track. About 45 minutes from Zinal, and just before coming to a white-walled hut, you will see a narrow path branching off to the right, signposted to Petit Mountet. (Grade 1 walk continues along the track, which leads directly to the cabane; for the Grade 2 walk take the narrow path.)

Following the footpath you reach another junction of paths five minutes later. Continue straight ahead. The path becomes quite delightful with views across the valley into the wild cwm headed by the Weisshorn. Among shrubbery the path drops into a narrow gully, crosses the stream and then climbs steeply onto the old moraine bank to reach the Cabane du Petit Mountet. *(Refreshments, accommodation. Note: reservations for overnight lodgings are obligatory. Telephone: 65 1380.)*

Route 51: **Zinal (1,675m)-Petit Mountet (2,142m)-**
                  Cabane du Mountet (2,886m)

Grade:	**3**
Distance:	**10kms**
Height gain:	**1,211 metres**
Time:	**5 hours**

Ober Gabelhorn (4063m) and the Zinal Glacier
The Weisshorn (4505m), seen from the path to the Mountet Hut

'It is worth a king's ransom to wander up into that world of towering crag and eternal snow, and lunch in the sunshine with sight regaled meanwhile by an almost unsurpassed prospect of stupendous peak, and glittering glacier.' So wrote G.D.Abraham of the amphitheatre of mountains seen from the Mountet Hut.

This approach entails the crossing of the Zinal Glacier on a marked route. The crossing is fairly straightforward, but the necessary safety precautions should be taken on account of hidden crevasses. For those neither equipped nor experienced enough to tackle the glacier crossing, it would be worthwhile following the route as far as Plan des Lettres, a grassy bluff a few minutes from the descent to the glacier. (This would be considered Grade 2-3.)

Follow Route 50 as far as the Cabane du Petit Mountet *(refreshments)* and continue along the crest of the moraine wall on a narrow and exposed path. As the moraine crumbles, the exact route is liable to change, but it will be well marked. It winds and climbs, sometimes with the aid of fixed ropes and chains as it crosses from the moraine to steep crags and slopes of rock and grass. In places there are metal ladders to aid the ascent or descent of a gully or two. Always the route is interesting and scenic. Returning to the moraine wall you come to the grassy bluff of the Plan des Lettres (2,465m) with its fabulous views to the cirque of peaks ahead, dominated by the Ober Gabelhorn. (A lovely place to laze in the sun and glory at the high mountain kingdom.)

Just beyond this point the trail drops to the glacier. Cross the glacier along a line of markers heading diagonally to the south-east. (About 40 minutes for the crossing.) The hut is then gained by following a path up the rocks on the far side to the south-facing ankles of Lo Besso. This most popular hut overlooks a world of snow and ice and rearing peaks. *(Refreshments.)* Allow 4½ hours for the return to Zinal.

Route 52:	Zinal (Sorebois) (2,438m)-Alp La Lé (2,184m)-Petit Mountet (2,142m)-Zinal (1,675m)

Grade:	2
Distance:	13kms
Height gain:	102 metres **Height loss:** 865 metres
Time:	4½ hours

Following a good high-level path along the western hillsides, this walk is forever interesting. Gazing across to the east one has views of Les

Ladder-aided path above Zinal

Diablons, the long ridge leading to Tête de Milon, then the steep walled Weisshorn and a crowd of glaciers hanging over a wild cirque. Far below the valley draws shadow, but ahead, coming ever closer, are those splendid peaks in the south.

112

Take the cable-car from Zinal to Sorebois, thus saving about two hours and more than 750 metres of ascent. The top station of the Sorebois lift occupies a landscape scarred by bulldozers to make ski pistes. Happily our path soon deserts this sorry place. On leaving the cable-car head south across the ski area (signposts) to join a broad track/ski piste for about 100 metres. When the track makes a right-hand bend find a narrow path dropping away to the left. A yellow arrow painted on a rock is your sign. The path now traverses the hill-side, crosses a stream by a wooden footbridge and continues ahead on an undulating course with lovely views across the valley.

After about 2 hours from Sorebois the path brings you to a grassy bluff where it forks. The left-hand path (yellow paint marks) descends towards Alp La Lé and Petit Mountet; that to the right leads up into a pleasant grassy cirque.

(Should you decide to take this alternative, you will find that the path fades after a while, and it will be necessary to make a traverse of the cirque - delightful and interesting - crossing streams and scree runs and rough pastures heading south, and then skirt round to the east in order to find a faint descending path that will bring you out near the Petit Mountet hut. Allow an additional 45 minutes for this diversion.)

Continuing along the main route the path makes a steady descent to the little hut of Alp La Lé (2,184m), and along to the Cabane du Petit Mountet *(refreshments, accommodation)*. Return to Zinal by the broad track winding downhill. (Allow 1¼ hours from Petit Mountet to Zinal.)

Route 53: Zinal (1,675m)-Sorebois (2,438m)

Grade:	2
Distance:	3.5kms
Height gain:	763 metres
Time:	1½-2 hours

A very steep walk to a fine viewpoint overlooking the Val de Zinal and its eastern wall, most of this climb takes place through forest.

From Zinal village find a narrow surfaced road leading down to the river near the tennis courts. Cross the river on a wooden bridge and bear right. In a few paces you will come to a junction of tracks. Our path continues ahead and is signposted. Heading through forest pass beneath the Zinal-Sorebois cableway and soon after an alternative path breaks away to Vernec and Pralong. The Sorebois path now climbs

View from Alp la Lé across Val d'Anniviers to the Weisshorn cirque

steeply among the trees, and after ignoring one or two alternative trails, comes out of the forest to tackle the steep grassy hillside beneath the cableway. Without diversion the route brings you to the cable-car station.

Routes from Sorebois:

There are several routes worth considering from the upper cable-car station. There's the southward trail to La Lé and **Petit Mountet** (Route 52); the northern path which goes past Tsirouc and down to **Grimentz** in the mouth of Val de Moiry (3 hours); another that descends to **Mottec** - halfway between Zinal and Ayer (about 1¼ hours); and the upward route to the viewpoint of **Corne de Sorebois** (2,890m 1¼ hours). From Corne de Sorebois a continuing path descends into the **Val de Moiry** to the west. See Route 59 below, which is given in the reverse direction.

Route 54: Zinal (1,675m)-Roc de la Vache (2,581m)-
Alp d'Ar Pitetta (2,248m)-Zinal

Grade:	2
Distance:	11kms
Height gain:	906 metres **Height loss:** 906 metres
Time:	5 hours

If I were to be restricted to only one day's walking in the whole of the Valais region, this is the walk I would choose. It has everything; an ever-varied vegetation, dashing streams and cascades, glistening little tarns, a high grassy col to cross, attractive and isolated alp huts along the route - and some of the most delectable mountain scenery one could possibly wish to see.

It's a steep haul up to Roc de la Vache, and a steep descent on the southern side, but the stunning views more than compensate for the labour involved. Since there are no opportunities for refreshment along the way, take a packed lunch and a flask of drink, set out early, walk slowly and absorb all the majesty of the mountains - and be thankful for the health and strength that enables you to achieve it.

Signs to look out for are initially to Cabane Tracuit and Roc de la Vache. Start by the church in Zinal, walk up a sloping narrow road along the left-hand side of it for about 60 metres where a track continues ahead. Bear right when you come to a surfaced road and walk along it, round a couple of hairpin bends, and then leave the road to head south along another track. Coming onto a second road for a few paces, you then leave this at a bend to continue along a footpath through woods. Cross a stream in a deep bed, then bear left along a road until you come to a narrow footpath on your right with a signpost pointing to Cabane Tracuit (5 hours) and Roc de la Vache (2½ hours).

Take this path to climb steeply among trees and shrubs and over rough pastures, and in about 50 minutes you will reach a tiny huddle of alp huts (2,061m). Continue above this alp. The path eases and becomes a superb belvedere along the steep mountainside with the valley more than 500 metres below, and with fine views ahead to the Bouquetins and Grand Cornier.

In 1 hour 45 minutes you will come above a waterfall to reach a junction of paths (2,500m) with a signpost. The path to Roc de la Vache (waymarked yellow) goes off to the right. (The left-hand fork goes up to Cabane Tracuit.)

About 15 minutes from the path junction you emerge onto the grassy saddle of Roc de la Vache (2½ hours from Zinal) with one of

Schalihorn (3974m), Pointe Sud de Moming (3963m) and the Moming Glacier, from Alp d'Ar Pitetta

the most glorious views imaginable. The valley is now some 900 metres below, but the eye is drawn by the glaciers stretching off to that amphitheatre of magnificence; shapely peaks stabbing the sky, ice walls like blue mirrors, snow slopes perfectly formed, cornices trapped in waves along the ridges; the contrast of height and depth, light and shade, white snow and brown rock, glacier and grass. Lo Besso holds back the tumultuous form of the Moming Glacier, with the Zinalrothorn nervously peering over and Pointe Sud de Moming next to it just coming into view. As we descend from this perch, so the cirque dominated by the Moming and Weisshorn glaciers spreads itself out for inspection on the left.

The descending path is clear, if narrow, and works its way down to the south, passes a deserted hut (Tsijiere de la Vatse, 2,388m) and continues to a collection of little tarns in an idyllic setting (3 hours from Zinal). Here the path forks again. The left branch goes up to Cabane d'Ar Pitetta, but ours heads off to the right, goes through a vegetated gully to another path junction with a signpost. Bear left to descend through a region of alpenroses, juniper and larch, still with lovely views ahead. Stay with the main path, ignoring an alternative *(difficile!)* leading to the right, and after a while you cross a glacial stream by way of a wooden bridge. Bear right at the next junction and follow the track down to Zinal.

Route 55:	Zinal (1,675m)-Combautanna (2,578m) Cabane de Tracuit (3,256m)

Grade:	3
Distance:	7kms
Height gain:	1,581 metres
Time:	5 hours

A steep ascent to reach the lofty position of a climbers' hut, this outing takes us into some wild country inhabited by marmots, with more magnificent views to enjoy.

Follow Route 54 as far as the junction of paths below the Roc de la Vache (2,500m 1¾ hours). Continue ahead (the left fork) up a slope where red-white paint marks lead the path. In 10 minutes or so you will come to the little alp hut of Combautanna (2,578m) - a splendid photogenic spot. The path leads on over a rolling pastureland up the left-hand (north) side of a bare amphitheatre that long ago lost its ice. Les Diablons stands above to the north, Tête de Milon forms the south-eastern bastion.

The path continues to work its way into the head of the amphitheatre, reaches a rocky area beneath the Diablon des Dames and makes a rising traverse to Col de Tracuit to reach the hut *(refreshments)*.

In good conditions the views are extensive and include Oberland peaks to the north, and far-off to the west, the big snowy mass of Mont Blanc. Climbs from here include Les Diablons, Bishorn and the north arête of the Weisshorn. Experienced mountain walkers undaunted by glacier work may descend to the Turtmanntal by way of the Turtmann Glacier or, more adventurously, to Randa in the Mattertal by way of the Bisjoch (between Bishorn and Brunegghorn). These are not routes to be considered, however, by the uninitiated or unequipped.

Route 56:	Zinal (1,675m)-Alp d'Ar Pitetta (2,248m)- Cabane d'Ar Pitetta (2,786m)

Grade:	2

Descent from Roc de la Vache. The deep trench carved by the Zinal Glacier is clearly seen below

Distance: 9kms
Height gain: 1,111 metres
Time: 4½ hours

From Alp d'Ar Pitetta (the 'little alp') the wanderer gazes up at the giant Weisshorn, at the hanging glaciers topped by the Schalihorn, Pointe Sud de Moming and Zinalrothorn. Lo Besso stands guard at the south-western end of the amphitheatre; Pointe d'Ar Pitetta is the northern sentry. In the heart of the cirque is the little climber's hut from which some of these peaks may be tackled. Its approach makes a grand day's walking, but note that as the hut has no guardian refreshments will not be available there.

Wander up-valley away from Zinal along the road, and where it ends continue ahead on a vague track. On coming to a bridge crossing the river go over to the western side to find a broad track heading south and steadily gaining height. (This is the route to Petit Mountet - Route 50.) Passing a small white-walled hut on your left you will soon come to a path going off to the left to cross the glacial stream seen pouring from the Pitetta cirque opposite. Follow this path to cross two streams and climb through a lush vegetation quite steeply up the hillside. When you come to a path junction with a route heading off to the left (marked *difficile*) continue ahead, but at the next junction bear right. This path leads through a vegetated gully and leads out to the tarns of Alp d'Ar Pitetta (about 2½ hours). This is a delectable spot, and worthy of a long spell of relaxation here.

Passing the tarns to your right ignore the path heading left (up to Roc de la Vache), and continue ahead now into the cirque, drawn by the huge shape of the Weisshorn ahead. It is a lovely bowl of mountain, and the path makes a steady ascent along the northern slopes to reach the hut set among the moraines tipped out by the retreating ice of the Glacier du Weisshorn. (Allow 3½ hours for the return to Zinal.)

Route 57: Grimentz (Barrage de Moiry) (2,249m)- A Lake Circuit

Grade: 1
Distance: 7kms
Height gain: 40 metres
Time: 1 hour 50 minutes

The reservoir of Lac de Moiry is fed by the meltwaters of the lovely Moiry Glacier at the head of the valley. By footpath along the bed of the Val de Moiry it will take about two hours from the flower-decked village of Grimentz to the dam, but it is possible, and recommended, to drive or take a Postbus from the village to the barrage. From there a pleasant and easy walk can be had around the lake.

At the eastern end of the barrage there is a Post Office, kiosk, restaurant and car park. Cross the dam to the western side and take a track heading left to bring you above the lake. You soon come to a junction with a signpost. Our footpath drops down half-left ahead and follows along the western side of the lake with grand views to the mountains at the head of the valley. On reaching the southern end, cross the stream by way of a footbridge, go up onto the road, bear left and follow this road back to the dam.

Route 58:   **Grimentz (Barrage de Moiry) (2,249m)-**
              Cabane de Moiry (2,825m)

Grade:	2
Distance:	7kms
Height gain:	576 metres
Time:	2½ hours

This route gives a splendid opportunity for walkers to intrude safely into the untamed heartland of the glacial mountain world. It treads along a narrow crest of moraine overlooking a chaos of an icefall, as dramatic as any likely to be found with such facility elsewhere in the Valais, and the view from the hut is indeed one of noble savagery.

From the car park at the Moiry barrage cross the dam and wander along the western shore of the lake (see Route 57 above). At the southern end of the lake go up onto the road and follow a continuing footpath over rough pastures, steadily gaining height on a rising traverse round the hillside towards the moraine wall forming the northern limits of the Moiry Glacier. The path leads up onto this moraine wall and along its narrow crest with views ahead of the great séracs and crevasses of the glacier. Before long it is necessary to descend from the crest down to the left and, still on the clear path, climb steeply a series of tight zig-zags up a great mound of rocks and boulders, on the top of which will be found the Moiry hut *(refreshments)*.

Above the hut to the south-east is the Col du Pigne, a little glacier pass which leads down to the pastures of La Lé. North of the hut, and reached by way of a steep gully, is the rocky Col de La Lé which also gives access to the same pastures. Opposite the hut, and across the glacier to the west, is Col de la Couronne (2,987m) by which Les

Moiry Glacier, below Cabane de Moiry

Haudères and the Val d'Hérens may be reached.

Route 59:   **Grimentz (Barrage de Moiry) (2,249m)-**
                    Col de Sorebois (2,896m)-Zinal (1,675m)

Grade: 2
Distance: 8kms
Height gain: 647 metres   **Height loss:**   1,221 metres
Time: 4 hours

A fine crossing of the ridge that divides Val de Moiry from Val de Zinal. It has to be said though, that while the views from the col are impressive, the actual pass itself is not, and the initial descent on the eastern side has been spoilt by bulldozed ski pistes.

At the eastern end of the Moiry dam an obvious path (almost a staircase) climbs the very steep slope to the high pastures overlooking the lake. It gains height quickly and without consideration for those who might be heavily laden, and about halfway to the pass is joined by another, older, path coming from the right. As you pause for a rest the views over Val de Moiry are very grand. The final haul up to the pass is over scree.

Col de Sorebois (2 hours from the dam) looks out over the Val de Zinal, and has superb views to the Weisshorn. Descend through a ski-ruined terrain to the Sorebois cable-car station, and from there take either of two signposted trails into the valley, passing through a region rich in wild flowers early in the summer, and finishing through steep forest.

| Route 60: | Grimentz (Barrage de Moiry) (2,249m)- |
| | Col de Torrent (2,919m)- Evolène (1,371m) |

Grade:	2		
Distance:	11kms		
Height gain:	670 metres	Height loss:	1,548 metres
Time:	5 hours		

Since the Moiry dam is easily accessible to motorists (and to travellers using the Postbus), the walk up to Col de Torrent on the ridge separating Val de Moiry from Val d'Hérens has become a popular excursion. This walk, which continues down into that lovely valley, makes an ideal link between two splendid villages. Grimentz is known for its flower-decked windows and crowded typically Valaisian chalets. Evolène is no less lovely, and in many respects might well stake a claim for the title of prettiest village in the Valais. By combining this walk with the crossing of Col de Couronne from Val d'Hérens back to Val de Moiry (see Route 61 below), an interesting two-day circular outing can be achieved.

From the car park and Postbus stop at the eastern end of the Barrage de Moiry, cross the dam to its western side and bear left along a signposted track. This leads up over grassy hillsides (signposted at path junctions) to reach the high tarn of Lac des Autannes (2,686m), two hundred metres or so below the pass.

Col de Torrent is reached after about 2 hours 45 minutes. Looking back there is a distant view of the Weisshorn, while off to the west the massing peaks include Pigne d'Arolla and Mont Blanc de Cheilon with Mont Blanc itself far off. (Given time and energy the summit of Sasseneire - 3,254m - to the north-west is accessible in about an hour or so.) On the western side the path drops steeply in zig-zags, passes a small tarn and swings down through Alp Cotter to reach the village of Villa (Villaz, 1,742m) perched on the hillside, about 1 hour 15 minutes below the pass. A road links this village (Postbus service) with Les

Haudères, but a footpath by the church plunges steeply down the slope to Evolène in the bed of the valley. *(Refreshments, accommodation, campsite, shops, banks, tourist information office.)*

Other Routes from Val de Moiry:

A walking holiday based on Grimentz offers a range of outings. The Postbus service allows a return to the village from most destinations, be they up-valley, along the Val d'Anniviers or even over the intervening ridges. Walks may be had through the woods that carpet the valley bed below the village heading towards the Moiry dam; or round the spur of mountain dividing Val de Moiry from Val de Zinal (Grimentz - Ayer; Grimentz - Zinal etc.). There is a long route (12kms) to be made along the hillsides heading north above Val d'Anniviers from Grimentz to **VERCORIN** near the mouth of the valley (allow 3½ hours); another crossing the ridge above the village to the west. By way of the **PAS de LONA** (2,787m) the walker can gain access to the village of Eison, north of Evolène in Val d'Hérens. This route is 13kms long and will take about 5½ hours to complete. And, finally, there is the more arduous crossing of **COL de la COURONNE,** (2,987m) to the west of the Cabane de Moiry, by which Les Haudères can be reached. This route is detailed in the reverse direction as Route 61 below.

Col de Riedmatten looking south-east

VAL d'HERENS

Position:	**South-east of Sion in the Rhône Valley.**
Map:	**L.S. 5006 'Matterhorn-Mischabel' 1:50,000**
	L.S. 5003 'Mont Blanc-Grand Combin'
	1:50,000 and/or
	L.S. 283 'Arolla' 1:50,000
Bases:	**Evolène (1,371m) Les Haudères (1,452m)**
	Arolla (1,998m)
Tourist Information:	**Office du Tourisme, 1968 Evolène**
	(Tel: 027 83 1235)
	Office du Tourisme, 1961 Les Haudères
	(Tel: 027 83 1015)
	Office du Tourisme, 1961 Arolla
	(Tel: 027 83 1083)

A great cluster of shapely peaks marks the head of the Val d'Hérens: Dent Blanche, Wandfluehorn, Tête Blanche, Mont Collon, Pigne d'Arolla. From them swirl long glacial tongues that project northward into the green swathe of pasture and forest where women still make hay dressed in traditional costumes, as they have for centuries. In the valley itself, and high on the eastern terrace of hillside, several villages maintain a close link with the past reluctant, it seems, to be drawn into the clamour for tourist favour which has brought about a rather faceless architectural style to some other areas. Traditions die hard in the Val d'Hérens, a valley that suffers less from the tourist invasion than many others, and where the walker can still find solitude among the high meadows and craggy passes that guard it.

The road into Val d'Hérens climbs out of the Rhône Valley by way of a series of zig-zags to reach the village of Vex, where it forks. Straight ahead the main road keeps above the left bank of the Borgne stream, while the right-hand road climbs again to Hérémence (with its extraordinary modern church - built 1971 - insulting the graceful timber buildings around it) and continues into the adjacent Val d'Hérémence as far as the huge Grande Dixence dam. The main Val d'Hérens road, meanwhile, continues to head south along the fertile

Pyramids d'Euseigne, Val d'Herens

hillside until it reaches the mouth of the Val d'Héremence where, with a tight hairpin, it crosses the Dixence and burrows through the curious Pyramids d'Euseigne. These lofty but slender pillars of earth and stone tower over the road, and are protected from the worst effects of erosion by the rocks that cap them and act as parasols.

Euseigne village sits among walnut trees, and soon after passing through it the road crosses to the right bank of the Borgne and steadily climbs up to the main village in the valley, Evolène. This is a delightful place, crowded as it is above soft pastures and with a lovely view to the Dent Blanche in the south-east. On the outskirts of the village there stands a huge memorial piton.

Les Haudères comes next, only 3.5 kilometres from Evolène and situated at the foot of the Dents de Veisivi, with the Val d'Arolla branching off to the south-west. The Val d'Hérens appears to be a minor spur here as it swings away to the south-east among more meadows and forest, but soon gives way to the sombre grey moraines and glaciers at the head of the valley.

The Val d'Arolla branch grows more narrow and steep-walled until, below the glorious north face of Mont Collon, a stupendous amphitheatre of peak and pasture and streaming ice-field catches the breath. Up here it's a world of enormous appeal to both climber and walker alike. Arolla is very much a mountaineering centre; it's not much of a village, but what is has on its doorstep makes it a place of great potential for all who love high mountains.

Main Valley Bases:
EVOLÈNE (1,371m) is a charming village of dark timber and stone houses squeezed above narrow alleyways. Hay barns stand beside shops in the one street, and there are flowers clustered at almost every window. Little kitchen gardens form neat squares behind some of the chalets; around the village meadows are shorn for hay, or grazed by cattle. Above rise the steep walls of the valley, but views to the south are full of promise. Several hotels offer accommodation in the modest one or two-star range. There is a campsite with excellent facilities. Evolène has restaurants, Post Office, banks, several food stores and other shops, and a tourist information office.
LES HAUDÈRES (1,436m) is caught in a triangle of roads to the south of Evolène. Attractive buildings, of the traditional Valaisian style, crowd the alleys. A little smaller than its neighbour, it has a few hotels (1, 2 and 3-star rated) and a campsite. Post Office, shops, tourist information office.
AROLLA (1,998m) is less attractive in itself than either Les Haudères or Evolène, but its setting is very fine with Mont Collon and Pigne d'Arolla nearby, and the steep wall opposite marked by the pinnacle of the Aiguille de la Tsa. This is very much the mountaineering centre of the valley, with accommodation to suit. There are a few hotels, some with dormitories, and houses offering apartments to rent. There is also a campsite below the village. Restaurants, limited shopping facilities (but including walking/climbing gear), tourist information bureau and a Post Office.

Other Valley Bases:
Above Evolène to the south-east there sits the idyllic little hamlet of **LA SAGE**, gazing over a splendid pastoral landscape with the big mountains hovering off to the south-west. It offers a limited hotel accommodation for those who wish to spend time in a fairly isolated position, while yet still being part of a community. And to the south-east of Les Haudères, on the route to Bricola and the Dent Blanche, **LA FORCLAZ** and **FERPÈCLE** are both mountaineering hamlets with hotel accommodation. Both have much of appeal about them.

Postbuses serve the whole valley.

Mountain Huts:

A small emergency bivouac hut for benighted climbers is situated on the Col de la Dent Blanche (3,540m), but this is not likely to be of practical interest to users of this guide. There is another hut for climbers on the lovely towering peak of Dent Blanche, accessible from Ferpècle via the Bricola alp in about 6 hours, and this is **CABANE de la DENT BLANCHE** (3,507m). Perched on a rocky spur below the south ridge of the mountain, and surrounded by glaciers, the hut has places for 40 people and a guardian for a brief summer period between mid-July and the beginning of September.

REFUGE des BOUQUETINS (2,980m) is another small hut (18 places, no guardian) tucked against the rocks bordering the Haut Glacier d'Arolla to the south-east of Mont Collon.

In the high wall of the Dents de Bertol, and approached from Arolla by way of a very steep haul of about 4 hours, there sits the **CABANE de BERTOL** (3,311m). Occupying an incredible position on the very ridge, this hut has a guardian from 1st July until the middle of September, and can sleep 80. Climbers' routes from here include the Aiguille de la Tsa to the north and the Bouquetins to the south. Experienced mountaineers can also set out from here to cross the Col d'Hérens to the Schönbiel hut, and continue down to Zermatt.

A little to the north-west of Cabane de Bertol the Société des Guides du Val d'Hérens has provided a hut on the west flank of Pointe des Genevois, some two hours' walk from Arolla. The **CABANE de la TSA** (2,607m) can sleep 60 in its dormitories, and is useful as a base for climbs on the various peaks prominent on the wall above.

CABANE des VIGNETTES (3,160m) is in another dramatic setting, squatting on a rocky ledge above the Col des Vignettes on the eastern shoulder of Pigne d'Arolla. A large and popular hut, it has spaces for almost 130 in its dormitories, and a guardian in residence from mid-March to mid-September. Suitable for climbs on Pigne d'Arolla, Mont Collon and L'Evêque, and for the crossing of a number of different cols. It is reached in about 3½ hours from Arolla on a marked glacier trail.

At the head of the Val des Dix - the upper stretches of Val d'Hérémence - and approached either by way of Arolla (4 hours) or the dammed Lac des Dix (3½ hours) is the large **CABANE des DIX** (2,928m). This hut can accommodate 145 in its dormitories, has a restaurant service and a guardian in occupation from mid-March until 15th September. Rising immediately behind it is the fabulous ice wall of the north face of Mont Blanc de Cheilon.

To the north of Cabane des Dix, and tucked in a rather barren side valley below the north-eastern glacier of Rosablanche, there sits **CABANE de PRAFLEURI** (2,624m), a hut suitable for energetic walkers bound upon a traverse of the Pennine Alps. Not owned by the Swiss Alpine Club, it can sleep 40, and has a guardian in residence during weekends only.

   CABANE des AIGUILLES ROUGES (2,810m) is in a landscape of rock overlooking the Val d'Arolla, the Veisivi-Bertol wall opposite, and to Mont Collon in the south. A fine hut with spaces for 80, it is reached in about 2½ hours from Arolla. A guardian is in residence during July and August. Climbs accessible from here include the Aiguilles Rouges d'Arolla, Mont de l'Etoile and Pointe de Vouasson.

Routes from Evolène:

Whilst the more attractive walks of the Val d'Hérens are to be had further to the south, Evolène has a number of recommended outings, ranging from the thirty minutes' stroll along the west side of the valley to the hamlet of **LANA** (1,407m), to the more arduous ridge crossings into neighbouring valleys. Of these, the crossing of **COL de TORRENT** (2,919m) into Val de Moiry is described above (Route 60) in the reverse direction. Heading west, over the ridge that separates Val d'Hérens from Val d'Hérémence, the **COL de la MEINA** (2,702m) gives a 6 hour walk from Evolène to Pralong. A little to the north of Col de la Meina, the summit of **PIC d'ARTSINOL** (2,998m) gives a broad panorama and makes a popular ascent from the valley - usually eased by taking a chair-lift from Lana to the alp of La Meina at 2,121 metres. Paths also head up the hillsides to reach a string of attractive villages settled upon a green terrace on the eastern side of the valley, while others follow along the bed of the valley to both north and south. The tourist information office in Evolène will happily sell you a special map with walking routes outlined upon it.

Route 61:   **Les Haudères (1,436m)-Col de la Couronne (2,987m)-Cabane de Moiry (2,825m)**

Grade:	3
Distance:	9kms
Height gain:	1,796 metres **Height loss:** 407 metres
Time:	5½ hours

This energetic route involves the crossing, not only of a high pass, but also of the Moiry Glacier. This glacier section, however, is taken at a fairly level and safe part of the ice-field below the hut. It should be stressed, though, that normal safety precautions must be taken. On the climb to the col the path leads through a flower-rich area, and views from the col itself are spectacular.

From Les Haudères either take the Postbus to La Forclaz (1,727m), or walk up by way of a signposted grassy footpath (about 1 hour). La Forclaz is an attractive little hamlet occupying a sunny position on the hillside above Les Haudères to the north-east. Leave the hamlet by way of a path near Café la Promenade heading south-east up the steeply sloping pastures. Cross a stream and continue through woods on a winding trail which takes you to a tiny huddle of alp huts at Bréona (2,197m). The trail continues to climb through high pastures with lovely views, and comes to another isolated alp, Remointse de Bréona (2,435m, 2 hours 15 mins). Beyond this the slope eases into the bowl of mountain headed by Couronne de Bréona, with the col a little below it to the right. When the path reaches a stream it crosses and heads to the right aiming for the pass. The final ascent to it involves a fairly steep haul.

Col de la Couronne is reached about 4 hours 15 minutes after leaving Les Haudéres, and a splendid high mountain view is the reward. Across the intervening ridge rise the great peaks of Val d'Anniviers, while below stretches the Moiry Glacier.

There is no real path on the eastern side of the pass, but traces of others having worked their way down. Cabane de Moiry is seen across the glacier. Make for the level section of glacier that forms a sort of plateau between icefall above and crevasse-tortured region below. In a normal summer you will find traces to follow. Cross directly to the rocks below the hut, with a rough path climbing to its perch. Cabane de Moiry *(refreshments)* is set in a dramatic position in full view of the great icefall. (See Val d'Anniviers section for full details.)

Route 62: Les Haudères (1,436m)-Col de Bréona (2,915m)-Les Haudères

Grade:	3
Distance:	12kms
Height gain:	1,479 metres **Height loss:** 1,479 metres
Time:	6½-7 hours

Another strenuous day's exercise, this route gives an opportunity to explore a little-visited corner of the mountains, and at the same time enjoy a magnificent panorama of gleaming high peaks. For much of the route we follow that which goes to Col de la Couronne. To save an hour's walk at the start of the day, it might be worth considering taking the Postbus to La Forclaz.

Follow directions as for Route 61 as far as the alp of Remointse de Bréona (2,435m, 2 hours 15 mins). Until this point the route is way-marked with paint flashes. Above the alp a ridge (marked Serra Neire on the map) slopes south-westward from the Col de Bréona, while the main ridge runs south-eastward rising to the summit of Couronne de Bréona and beyond that, dips to the pass crossed in Route 61.

Head up the slope to the north-east for about 10 minutes to reach a broad track. Follow this to the right until it forks after several hundred metres where you turn left, to head north on another track which leads up the slope. When this forks bear left again (north-wards). This track goes up to a flower-decked meadow caught between the enclosing arms of the ridge, with lovely views and an air of isolation.

Above, the ridges to west and east have contrasting features, craggy on one side, smooth on the other. The path leads on heading north and climbs steeply to the pass (4 hours from La Forclaz), a nick in the junction of ridges where superb views gaze out at the big snow and ice-capped mountains of Val d'Anniviers and, south-westward, to Pigne d'Arolla and its neighbours. (Allow 2½ hours for the descent.)

Route 63:   **Ferpècle (Salay) (1,766m)-Bricola (2,415m)-Ferpècle**

Grade:	2
Distance:	6kms
Height gain: 649 metres	**Height loss:** 649 metres
Time:	2½ hours

Bricola alp is one of those marvellous green belvederes from which the walker is enabled to gaze directly onto some stunning mountain scenery. Steeply below runs the Glacier de Ferpècle from a tumble of séracs. Opposite rises the dark peak of Mont Miné, with the Mont Miné ice-field pouring alongside it. Above this glacier rears the great mountain wall that supports the Veisivi peaks, Pointe des Genevois and the needle-like Aiguille de la Tsa. At the head of the Ferpècle glacier dazzle Tête Blanche and Wandfluehorn, while soaring so dramatically overhead is the huge cone of Dent Blanche. Bricola makes a wonderful site for a picnic, but note that there are no refreshments to be bought there.

Take the Postbus or drive from Les Haudères to the tiny hamlet of

Glacier du Mont Miné, from the path to Bricola

Ferpècle, which lies about 7 kilometres away to the south-east. It is an ever-interesting ride, full of colour and contrasts, and with the great shape of Dent Blanche so enticing ahead. (From La Forclaz a meadow path leads to Ferpècle in about 45 minutes.)

At the entrance to the hamlet there is a little parking area to the left of the road by a large boulder. Our footpath begins here, heading up the slope to the left of Hotel du Col d'Hérens, climbing among trees to pass behind a wall surrounding a chapel. The path then breaks away to the right along the hillside among trees and shrubs and flowers. After crossing two streams you come to a junction of paths (35 minutes). Having now left the woods take the footpath signposted to Cabane Rossier.

The path is clear all the way to Bricola. It climbs in steady twists up the hillside aiming south-east with lovely views to the glaciers ahead. There are one or two steep sections with tight zig-zags, but mostly the path maintains a steady rising traverse. After about 1½ hours from Ferpècle it brings you onto the green plateau of Bricola with a tall stone building standing on the edge of the alp, and a number of derelict shepherds huts lying in ruins nearby. (Allow 1 hour for the return to Ferpècle.)

Note: Two extensions may be made from Bricola to lengthen the outing and to explore some more fine scenery. The first is to **LES MANZETTES** on the route to Cabane de la Dent Blanche, and is reached by taking the broad path leading south-east from the tall three-storey building. It takes you over a sparse region of boulder-pocked pastures and, in an hour or so, leads to the moraine crest between the Manzettes and Ferpècle glaciers. The view of the glaciers is very fine from here.

The second route extension takes us up to a high wild cwm below the **WEST FACE OF DENT BLANCHE**. This would be graded 3. As with the above extension take the broad path leading south-east from the tall building at Bricola, but on reaching a fast-running stream with a wooden footbridge over it, leave the main path and head up the slopes to the left, signposted to the bivouac hut on the Col de la Dent Blanche. A faint path gives way to cairns and paint flashes. It climbs steeply, for much of the way following the stream, and brings you into a shallow 'gully' walled on the left by a moraine crest. At the head of this is a very wild landscape littered with large boulders. Bear half-right up this towards an obvious col, then veer right to get onto a ridge which overlooks the grand glacier-clad country to the south. The Dent Blanche to the south-east looks formidable, if somewhat foreshortened from here. (About 50 minutes from Bricola.) Return to the gully and descend with care to Bricola.

Route 64: **Les Haudères (1,436m)-Veisivi (1,877m)-**
Roc Vieux (2,213m)

Grade:	2
Distance:	6kms
Height gain:	777 metres
Time:	2½ hours

Immediately above Les Haudères to the south the mountains rise up to form the long dividing wall between Val d'Arolla and the final stretch of Val d'Hérens (Val d'Ferpècle). The little peak at the very end of this long wall is known as Roc Vieux. It's a noted viewpoint.

Take the Arolla road out of Les Haudères and shortly after rounding the sharp right-hand bend leave the road for a footpath on the left. It follows along the forest edge for a while, then begins to rise among the trees and, about 4 kilometres from the village, emerges from the forest at the huddle of alp huts of Veisivi. Through this the path works its way across the meadows towards the east, begins to climb steeply, then veers north-eastwards. Roc Vieux is reached in a little under an hour from the alp huts.

Route 65:   Arolla (1,998m)-Pra Gra (2,479m)

Grade:	**1-2**
Distance:	**2.5kms**
Height gain:	**481 metres**
Time:	**1 hour**

Pra Gra must be one of the loveliest alps in all of Switzerland. Standing on a green terrace overlooking a wonderland of peaks, pastures and glaciers, the collection of grey stone-roofed chalets, barns and cattle byres makes an idyllic setting for a photograph. Mont Collon looks exceedingly grand from here. So does Pigne d'Arolla. The big wall from which juts the Aiguille de la Tsa blocks the view to the east, but is far enough away to give a full impression of its stature. The walk itself has sufficient steep sections to make the arrival at Pra Gra very welcome, and on the approach it is tempting to keep stopping to catch another view of Mont Collon growing in the south.

From the main square near the Post Office in Arolla walk uphill along the surfaced road on a sign to Lac Bleu. Ignore the first footpath heading towards Lac Bleu near the 'Centre Alpen' and continue for two more hairpin bends. At the second of these break away to the right along a broad track that winds steadily uphill across steeply sloping pastures. Keep above a small huddle of alp huts and continue to gain height. There are path sections to avoid some of the long loops of the track (signposts indicate the route to Cabane des Aiguilles Rouges, which is the route we take). Eventually you come onto the shelf of hillside with Pra Gra seen to the left.

Route 66:   Arolla (1,998m)-Cabanes des Aiguille Rouges (2,810m)-Lac Bleu (2,090m)-La Gouille (1,845m)

Grade:	**2-3**		
Distance:	**10kms**		
Height gain:	**812 metres**	**Height loss:**	**965 metres**
Time:	**4 hours**		

A strenuous but fine walk to a mountain hut with superb views, followed by a very steep descent. On the ascent the route takes us by the alp huts of Pra Gra, then over a wild patch of mountain country

*The lovely alp of Pra Gra above Arolla, Mont Collon in the
background*

marked by streams and boulders and screes to gain the hut on its lofty
perch. Refreshments are available at the hut, and it is worth taking the
whole day over the walk to enjoy its many different aspects without
being pressured by the march of time.

Follow Route 65 as far as Pra Gra (1 hour) and continue to the right
of the alp along a clear broad path heading north across pastures to a
wide plateau. Here the path swings left into a wild region of boulder
slopes and gravel beds with streams running through. At the head of
this minor hanging valley lie snow slopes and a small glacier, with the
Col des Ignes tucked below the summit of La Cassorte. The path veers
to the right to cross more boulder slopes and scree, and on a short
exposed section a fixed chain gives reassurance. (This is not really
difficult or dangerous except when icy.) The final ascent to the hut is
rather steep, but not unduly arduous. The Cabane des Aiguilles
Rouges *(refreshments)* is reached in about 2½ hours.

To descend to Lac Bleu, continue above the hut for a short stretch
(direction arrows painted on the rocks), then drop steeply, first to the
east to cross a stream, then swing south-eastwards on a clear path.
This is a very steep and tiring descent, but interesting all the way as

Cabane des Aiguille Rouges, Aiguille de la Tsa in the background

you go down through the various layers of vegetation. The path brings you to the little tarn of Lac Bleu which has a waterfall cascading into its western end.

At the eastern end of the lake the path continues, passes to the side of the huts of Louché and descends among pine woods to the valley road at La Gouille *(refreshments)*. Take the Postbus back to Arolla.

Route 67: Arolla (1,998m)-Plan Bertol (2,664m)-Cabane de Bertol (3,311m)

Grade:	**3**
Distance:	**7kms**
Height gain:	**1,313 metres**
Time:	**4-5 hours**

Only those with experience and the necessary equipment to tackle the steep little Glacier de Bertol should attempt the full ascent to the hut. However, a worthwhile walk could be taken as far as the edge of the glacier above Plan Bertol for those unable to go as far as the hut. This would be Grade 2.

Go down the road from Arolla's square and, instead of taking the sharp left-hand bend as for Les Haudères, bear right along the surfaced road heading south towards Mont Collon. When the surfacing ends continue ahead along the gravel road, pass a works cableway on your right and keep ahead. When you reach a wooden bridge with a metal rail leading over the stream to the left, cross over and bear left. The path climbs in zig-zags and heads south-east towards Mont Collon. On reaching a path junction at 2,336 metres bear left (direction sign) and climb into the hanging valley carved out by the Bertol Glacier long ago. Continue through this, passing Plan de Bertol and going up to a small stone-built hut with splendid views overlooking Mont Collon and its crevassed glacier in the south-west. (About 3 hours; allow 1½ hours for the return to Arolla.)

On coming to the edge of the Glacier de Bertol head diagonally across it to the north-east to pass beside a rocky islet. The glacier is steep and crevassed and requires caution. The final steep haul to the hut is aided by a fixed cable.

Cabane de Bertol *(refreshments)* enjoys a wonderful panorama dominated by the great sea of ice of the Mont Miné and Ferpècle glaciers to the east. For details of accommodation, period when guardian is in residence etc., see introductory section above.

North Face of Mont Blanc de Cheilon (3870m).
Cabane des Dix sits below this on the glacier's left bank.

Route 68: **Arolla (1,998m)-Pas de Chèvres (2,855m)-Cabane des Dix (2,928m)**

Grade:	**3**
Distance:	**6kms**
Height gain: 950 metres	**Height loss: 100 metres**
Time:	**4-4½ hours**

Both this and Route 69 below, cross the high ridge dividing Val d'Arolla and Val des Dix, but in opposite directions. The two passes, Pas de Chèvres and Col de Riedmatten, are situated within a few metres of each other and consequently enjoy very similar views. Gazing south-west we look upon the fabulous north face of Mont Blanc de Cheilon; to the south-east we have Mont Collon dominating, with the tip of the Matterhorn seen poking above the horizon.

Cabane des Dix sits on the left bank of the Glacier de Cheilon with the huge wedge of Mont Blanc de Cheilon looming overhead. To reach it from the pass involves a novel descent down fixed ladders followed by the crossing of the glacier. At the point of crossing the glacier is mostly level and untroubled, but the usual safety precautions should be taken.

Walk up the road from Arolla's village square for a short distance and turn left along a footpath leading to the Grand Hotel and Kurhaus. The path beyond this is marked with yellow paint flashes and is signposted. Heading up a series of zig-zags you work your way over steep grassy slopes to join a broad track. Signs are for both Pas de Chèvres and Col de Riedmatten.

The track winds on, and there are delightful views overlooking Mont Collon and Pigne d'Arolla. Pass a clutch of derelict huts on the left and continue to climb among pastures heading south-west. After some time you cross a stream on a wooden bridge (2,512m) and follow a rough road for a few metres before breaking away left on a footpath climbing below a green bank with Pigne d'Arolla making a superb backcloth beyond it. Looking back there are views of the great Glacier de Tsijiore Nouve sweeping valley-wards, and Mont Collon standing proud.

In a bowl of undulating pastures pocked with boulders and with streams running through, a path forks. To the right lies the route to Col de Riedmatten, but ours is the left-hand trail and it soon brings us to the Pas de Chèvres. A marvellous panorama opens ahead. Take care on the descent of the ladders, and at the foot of them follow the path to the glacier's edge. The route across the ice will most likely be clear, and any crevasses easily detected. But take precautions anyway. On the western side a path climbs to the hut *(refreshments)*.

Route 69: Le Chargeur (2,102m)-Col de Riedmatten (2,919m)-Arolla (1,998m)

Grade:	2-3		
Distance:	14kms		
Height gain:	817 metres	**Height loss:**	921 metres
Time:	5½ hours		

This is a grand day's walk. It begins at the world's tallest dam, wanders alongside a lake, climbs into some wild rough countryside with beautiful views, crosses a lofty pass with a glorious panorama of the mountains that virtually encircle Arolla, and descends through a landscape of grass and glacier. There are no opportunities for refreshment along the way, so wait for a fine clear day, take a packed lunch and bottled drink and walk at an even pace to allow plenty of time to soak in the views and to study the flowers along the way.

The walk begins in the next valley to the west of Val d'Hérens; the Val d'Hérémence. Take a bus to the dam at Le Chargeur. (Note that

Pigne d'Arolla (3796m)

the bus service through Val d'Hérémence is privately operated. Take the Postbus Arolla-Vex, and change at Vex for the private bus to Le Chargeur. Alternatively, Postbus to Euseigne and walk the linking road into Val d'Hérémence to catch the last stage of the bus ride at Maché.) There is an hotel at Le Chargeur and a cable-car to the top of the dam wall, thereby saving a steep climb (30 minutes or so) up a twisting narrow path.

From the western end of the Grande Dixence dam walk along the right-hand side of the lake on a clear broad track which soon passes through several tunnels. The first of these is the longest and darkest, but is lit by electric lights. A switch at the entrance to the tunnel gives you 5 minutes of light. As you wander alongside the lake there are lovely views to the high peaks ahead.

At the southern end of Lac des Dix you come to a metal suspension footbridge which crosses the south-eastern inlet. It is a slender but safe bridge (likely to upset those who suffer from vertigo!) and leads to a steel staircase and a small works building. From here a narrow path climbs some steep grass slopes (good for wild flowers) and leads into the valley carved by the Cheilon glacier. This valley broadens considerably farther south, but initially it is narrow and littered with boulders. The path works its way along the left-hand side of it, over boulder slopes and across streams, then zig-zags to gain some height. All the time Mont Blanc de Cheilon gleams ahead, its glacier and long trough of moraine sweeping through the valley below. After a fairly lengthy level stretch the path suddenly swings to the east and climbs steeply to gain the narrow notch of Col de Riedmatten (4 hours from Le Chargeur).

This is a classic rocky pass and the views from it are superb. Mont Collon impresses to the south-east, as does the Dent Blanche. The Matterhorn's summit can be seen on the skyline, and the impression one gains is of a well-ordered landscape, one of the finest to be enjoyed by the walker in the Pennine Alps. (For an even broader panorama, follow the narrow trail heading left onto the ridge for a few minutes. But take care, it requires a little scrambling in places.)

Descending to the east the path is clearly defined, but rather steep at first. It leads into a bowl of mountainside to join the path from Pas de Chèvres, and then swings on down the long sloping pastures all the way to Arolla, enjoying more lovely views en route.

Other Walks in Val d'Hérémence:

Val d'Hérémence offers peaceful walking in green countryside; high valley walks, passes to cross, mountain bluffs to traverse, water-courses to follow. These water-courses are known in the Valais region as *bisses*. Wooden conduits have been constructed and ditches dug to lead streams along otherwise summer-dry mountainsides in order to irrigate crops. Footpaths follow these to facilitate occasional mainten-ance work on them, or as a means of farmers moving from one parcel of land to another. One such is the **BISSE d'ERNAYA** which links the Val d'Hérémence with Val d'Hérens. It begins by the Dixence stream at Leteygeon (1,559m) and swings round the northern hillside separating the two valleys, to finish at La Luette (997m) in Val d'Hérens south of Euseigne.

Another *bisse* route, **ANCIEN BISSE de VEX**, runs from Mayens de Sion (high on the western hillside near the mouth of Val d'Hérens) south to Planchouet and Lavanthier. Postbus routes serve villages at both ends of this walk.

A 14 kilometre walk may be taken from **PRALONG** (camping) below the Grand Dixence dam northwards to Veysonnaz above the Rhône Valley. (About 4 hours.) There's also the crossing of **COL de la MEINA** (2,702m) which leads a route from Pralong over to Evolène; and numerous other walking possibilities. Study the map for inspiration.

At the heart of Val de Nendaz, looking towards Col de Prafleuri

VAL de NENDAZ

Position:	South of the Rhône Valley, and west of Val d'Hérémence.
Maps:	L.S. 5003 'Mont Blanc-Grand Combin' 1:50,000 L.S. 273 'Montana' 1:50,000
Bases:	Haute Nendaz (1,365m) Super Nendaz (1,733m)
Tourist Information:	Office du Tourisme, 1961 Haute Nendaz (Tel: 027 88 1444)

Val de Nendaz is one of the smallest of the southern glens to flow into the Rhône. It's soft and distinctly pastoral without the rugged or towering ice-adorned peaks that so characterise the major valleys farther east. That being said it is, nevertheless, a vale of great charm and with some lovely walks to be had in it.

The valley projects from an open sunny terrace high above the Rhône, and is reached by way of a road that climbs among orchards of peach and apricot for sixteen kilometres or so from Sion to Haute Nendaz. On the drive up the hillside long views are shown down through the valley of the Rhône and across to the Oberland peaks that form a great wall to the north. It leads to the bright terrace of neat chalets and shorn meadows, but beyond the scattered village of Haute Nendaz the valley slices to the south, forest-draped, pasture-trim and gentle. One or two hay barns and chalets stand in the tree-shrouded meadows, then as the forest thins and the valley opens, the modern ski resort of Super Nendaz is reached.

More meadows stretch to the south and the valley forks. To the south-west streams flow down from the high snows of Mont Gelé and Mont Fort, but the main branch leads to the dammed Lac de Cleuson where the road ends. Beyond the lake the valley veers south-eastwards into a lost sanctuary headed by the snowy mass of Rosablanche and its ice-field known as the *Grand Desert*. Up here a great knot of peaks makes a formidable wall, to the east of which lies Lac des Dix and the Val d'Hérémence. Another world.

Nendaz has a number of mechanical aids (at Nendaz Station) to service a growing winter tourist trade, and Super Nendaz (or Siviez) gives access to a large area of ski terrain with chair-lifts, cable-cars and tows. But there are still plenty of footpaths away from such mechanised intrusions. Footpaths that follow irrigation *bisses*, that wind along high sloping pastures and among masses of wild flowers into a peaceful, tranquil region.

Val de Nendaz is quietly unassuming, quietly lovely. It is worth a visit.

Main Bases:

HAUTE NENDAZ (1,365m) gazes across the broad swathe of the Rhône Valley to the heights of the Bernese Alps. Occupying a sunny terrace above orchard-rich hillsides, it gives no true impression of the pleasant valley hidden among pine forests behind it. The village has several hotels in the middle-quality range. There are limited shopping facilities, but there is a tourist information office, and Haute Nendaz is served by Postbus from Sion.

SUPER NENDAZ (1,733m), which is also known as Siviez, stands deep inside the Val de Nendaz and, apart from the little alp hamlet of Les Chottes on the hillside above, is the only settlement to do so. But perhaps it is wrong to describe this collection of hotels and apartment blocks as a settlement. It is a specially-built tourist development which has opened the valley to the downhill-ski industry. In summer there are apartments to rent. There is a restaurant and the resort is served by Postbus.

Mountain Huts:

The Swiss Alpine Club has only one hut accessible from Val de Nendaz, and that is situated on the Val de Bagnes slope of the mountains to the south-west. **CABANE du MONT FORT** (2,457m) may be reached from Super Nendaz by way of either Col de Chassoure and Col des Vaux, or via Col du Mont Gelé. There is a cable-car route to Col des Gentianes which also grants access to the hut by way of a service road. The hut has places for 100, a full meals service and a guardian during the spring months of April and May for skiers on the *haute route*, and during July and August for climbers and walkers.

There is another hut, **REFUGE de ST. LAURENT** (2,485m), which is situated a little to the south of Lac de Cleuson below Rosablanche and the Grand Desert. Regret no further details to hand.

Route 70:   Super Nendaz (1,733m)-Lac de Cleuson (2,186m)-
Super Nendaz

Grade:	2
Distance:	11kms
Height gain:	594 metres **Height loss:** 594 metres
Time:	4 hours

Walking along this high path on the eastern side of the valley we gain views to the mountains rising in the south, and look down onto lush pastures leading to the dammed lake. There are woodlands and shrubs and plenty of wild flowers along the route of the path, which also follows the course of a long-disused *bisse* - of which there are few signs remaining.

The path begins on the right bank of the stream, in the north-eastern corner of the car park at Super Nendaz, and climbs in zig-zags to the little alp hamlet of Les Chottes (1,858m, 15 minutes). This attractive huddle of chalets and barns is a complete contrast to the modern buildings below. Overhead swings a chair-lift. Head south (to the right) on the track which runs along the hillside (not that which slopes down into the valley again!) steadily gaining height through forest shade. After about 1,500 metres from Les Chottes the path climbs steeply in zig-zags with views opening to the south, and comes to a signpost (2,260m 1 hour 15 mins). Bear right here along a level path which is the course of the *Ancien Bisse de Chervé*.

Follow this footpath, which is narrow in places, as it traverses the hillside among shrubs and flowers, the mountains ahead looking grand, the barrage of Lac de Cleuson coming clearly into view below. Continue beyond the southern end of the lake until the path forks and you can descend towards a narrow stretch of valley where there is a signpost (about 2½ hours). Bear right and wander back along the track above the lake to reach the barrage at its northern end.

From the dam to Super Nendaz will take a little over an hour. Either descend directly along the road leading from the dam, or break away from it to the left on a footpath that goes through the woods and across pastures on the western side of the valley, and also arrives back in Super Nendaz.

Other Walks in Val de Nendaz:

The route of the **ANCIEN BISSE de CHERVÉ**, partially followed on Route 70 but which extends for almost 13 kilometres, may be walked in its entirety from Thyon 2000 (Postbus from Sion) to Lac de

Cleuson. A fine hillside traverse, this would occupy about 4 hours. There is another *bisse* route, **ANCIEN BISSE du MILIEU**, which links Haute Nendaz with the village of Veysonnaz on the hillside at the eastern entrance to the valley. Walking this path will take about 3½ hours. From Haute Nendaz it cuts into the initial stages of Val de Nendaz, then returns along the opposite hillside.

From the southern end of Lac de Cleuson a footpath continues via the St. Laurent hut to **LAC du GRAND DESERT**; another heads south-eastwards to cross **COL de PRAFLEURI** (2,965m 4½ hours) and descends then to the hanging valley above Lac des Dix where the **CABANE de PRAFLEURI** (2,932m 6 hours) will be found. The energetic and experienced walker could use this as a stage in a traverse of the Pennine Alps.

The map shows several accessible passes crossing the various ridges that make up the amphitheatre at the head of Val de Nendaz. By linking one or two of these, adventurous circuits could be made. But for the less committed of walkers there are plenty of valley paths that lead through woods and over soft pastures to satisfy several days of a holiday based here.

VAL de BAGNES

Position:	**South of the Rhône, approached from Martigny.**
Map:	**L.S. 5003 'Mont Blanc-Grand Combin' 1:50,000**
Bases:	**Sembrancher (717m) Verbier (1,490m) Fionnay (1,490m)**
Tourist Information:	**Office du Tourisme, 1933 Sembrancher (Tel: 026 8 8621)**
	Office du Tourisme, 1936 Verbier (Tel: 026 7 7181)
	Office du Tourisme, 1931 Fionnay (Tel: 026 7 1322)
	Office Régional du Tourisme, Place Centrale 9, 1920 Martigny (Tel: 026 2 1018)

Val de Bagnes makes a startling contrast to the valley of the Rhône, for whilst the Rhône is a broad, flat-bottomed trench with vines and orchards on its slopes, the valley of the Drance is deep and narrow with rugged sides and alps high above. At first, as the visitor makes his entrance from Martigny, there's a brave extension of Rhône Valley husbandry as vineyards terrace the hillsides. Then the walls of the valley are squeezed to form a defile, dark and oppressive, raw and seemingly lifeless until they open again at Sembrancher where the Drance d'Entremont comes rushing from the south to join the Drance de Bagnes on the edge of the village.

From here to the roadhead at the huge dam of Mauvoisin, some 24 kilometres away, Val de Bagnes makes a long curve to the south-east, growing ever more wild and with the mountains closing in. There are places where the floor of this valley is temporarily flat and broad enough to allow cultivation. There are small timber chalets in village clusters and green meadows cut in patterns or neatly shorn by cattle, but the deeper one travels into its recesses the less likely it is to find level ground, and there are times especially in bad weather - when the

very tightness of the constricting walls creates an overpowering sense of disquiet.

Above the dammed Lac de Mauvoisin a fresh horizon is revealed; a landscape of big mountains and glaciers with the huge mass of the Grand Combin (4,314m) to the west, the easy peak but superb viewpoint of La Ruinette (3,875m) and Mont Blanc de Cheilon

(3,870m) to the east. There are some good wild walks to be had here.

Curling from the snowfields of La Ruinette and Mont Blanc de Cheilon is the Glacier du Giétro, a much-reduced ice-sheet from that which was responsible for blocking the valley in 1818. In that year a great mass of ice fell away from the glacier, damming the gorge and creating a natural lake behind it. When the ice-dam was burst the wall of water that swept through the valley killed 34 people and caused considerable damage to buildings, trees and cattle. Today the great concrete dam of Mauvoisin stands some 237 metres high. It took over two million cubic metres of cement and eight year of work to build.

But elsewhere in the Val de Bagnes there are high hillside shelves and ice-scooped plateaux now turned to pasture where tourist villages and remote alp hamlets perch full in the sun with extensive views over the walling peaks of the valley, and off to the snows of Mont Blanc hovering not so very far away.

Main Bases:
SEMBRANCHER (717m) is in a good position to explore other valleys besides that of Bagnes, since it sits at the entrance to Val d'Entremont. A small stone-walled village with limited hotel accommodation, it does however boast two campsites and a tourist information office, a handful of food stores and a restaurant. It is served by Postbus and railway.
VERBIER (1,490m) is well-known as a winter sports resort. It perches high above the valley on a broad shelf of hillside overlooking the Grand Combin massif, a sprawl of hotels, apartment blocks and chalets. There are numerous mechanical devices swinging up to the high ridges above, lacing the peaks and pastures in giant webs of cable. There is no shortage of accommodation: some 38 hotels and 1,200 chalets or flats to let. Verbier has a tourist information office, shops, banks, restaurants and numerous facilities provided for the holiday maker. It is reached by an extremely steep road that climbs in tight hairpins (Postbus), and also by way of a cable-car from Le Châble.
FIONNAY (1,490m) has long been used as a mountaineering centre, though it seems to have grown hardly at all. It has the advantage for those travelling on a shoestring in that the village has two sets of dormitory accommodation, in addition to hotel and *pension*. The staff at the tourist office will give advice on prices.

Other Valley Bases:
Most of the remaining villages in Val de Bagnes offer some holiday accommodation. At **BRUNSON** there is a Youth Hostel as well as *pension*, and at nearby **Le CHÂBLE** there are several small hotels. There are campsites at **CHAMPSEC**, about four kilometres upstream of Le Châble, and also on the outskirts of **BONATCHESSE**, the last hamlet in the valley. At **MAUVOISIN** below the dam there is an hotel with restaurant.

Postbuses run throughout the valley, and a railway from Martigny goes as far as Le Châble.

Mountain Huts:
Three SAC huts in the area may be of interest to users of this guide. There are one or two smaller bivouac huts set high in the mountains, but these are primarily for the use of benighted climbers. **CABANE du MONT FORT** (2,457m) has already been mentioned under Val de Nendaz section above. It has places for 100 in its dormitories, and a guardian in residence during the spring ski-touring season (April/May), as well as in July and August. At other times it is open at weekends, but prior reservations are essential. Meals and drinks are available when the guardian is there. The hut, set on the western slopes of Mont Fort, is easily accessible from Verbier by way of road and track, or by path in about 3 hours.

At the head of the valley to the east of Grand Combin, **CABANE de CHANRION** (2,462m) is delightfully situated among high pastures with little tarns nearby, and with lovely views. This too has bedspace for 100 and a full meals service available when the guardian is in occupation. This is in the ski-touring season (the hut is one of the overnight resting places for those attempting the classic *haute route* from Chamonix to Zermatt), and in summer from July to September. Many fine high glacier passes are made accessible by use of the Chanrion hut, as well as ascents of La Ruinette, Pointe d'Otemma, which rises directly behind it, Mont Blanc de Cheilon, Pigne d'Arolla, Mont Avril, Mont Gelé, etc.

On the right bank of the large Glacier de Corbassière to the south of Fionnay, and reached from the village by way of a four-hour approach path, is the **CABANE de PANOSSIÈRE** (2,669m). With places for 100 in its dormitories, and a guardian in residence during April, May and July to the middle of September when meals are available, it is a popular hut with ski-tourers, climbers and adventurous mountain walkers. A number of interesting expeditions are possible from its base.

Route 71:   Verbier (1,490m)-Cabane du Mont Fort (2,457m)

Grade:	2
Distance:	7kms
Height gain:	967 metres
Time:	3 hours

The green bowl of mountainside on which the teeming resort of Verbier is set is strung about with numerous mechanical devices -

primarily for winter sports enthusiasts. However, the views cast from it are splendid indeed, gazing off to the Grand Combin and many other lovely snow-capped peaks that create a glistening, if ragged, skyline. From some areas it is possible to see Mont Blanc and the Dents du Midi, while the Val de Bagnes yawns as a deep and hollow gulph below. There are many kilometres of footpath winding around the pastures and forests of this bowl. Some cross easy passes into Val de Nendaz, others head down to the valley of the Rhône or along the hillside above Val de Bagnes. This particular walk makes for an easy approach to the Mont Fort hut. If taken as a round-trip, allow a little over two hours for the return to Verbier.

From the main, or central, square of Verbier walk along Route de Médran guided by signposts indicating the route to Clambin. These lead uphill on Rue de Tintaz, then along a gravel path heading between some chalets. This in turn leads onto a dirt track which goes to the hamlet of Clambin (1,844m) where a sign points left to Les Ruinettes and Cabane du Mont Fort. Ther path takes you up into woods, climbing steeply in zig-zags and then out to open ski-terrain. Passing near the top station of Les Ruinettes gondola lift (2,195m, 2 hours, *refreshments*) the marked way continues to gain height, but much more gently now heading south-east with a splendid panorama of big mountains hovering off to the south and the west. Then, rounding a bluff, the hut comes into sight and is reached without difficulty. *(Refreshments available.)*

Walking Routes from Cabane du Mont Fort:

This hut allows access to several passes that could be crossed by energetic walkers. By traversing north-westwards there is a way over Les Attelas (west of Mont Gelé) to the **LAC des VAUX**, then from there go west to cross Col des Mines and descend to Verbier. From the hut to Verbier by this route would take about 3½ hours.

COL des GENTIANES is easily reached by way of a broad track from the hut, and from the north side cableways lead up to Mont Fort (3,329m) or down to Tortin in Val de Nendaz. Similarly **COL du MONT GELÉ**, almost due north of the hut, is reached in one hour, and a descent may be made via a small tarn to Tortin, and from there down to Super Nendaz. This would take about four hours from the hut.

Another crossing, this time of Col de Louvie, the Grand Desert glacier below Rosablanche, and then Col de Prafleuri, makes a day's walk of 6 hours to **CABANE de PRAFLEURI** above Val d'Hérémence, and is useful for those involved in a traverse of the southern valleys.

Route 72: **Verbier (1,490m)-Cabane du Mont Fort (2,470m)-Col Termin (2,648m)-Lac de Louvie (2,213m)-Fionnay (1,490m)**

Grade: 3
Distance: 16kms
Height gain: 1,158 metres   **Height loss:** 1,158 metres
Time: 8½ hours

This long and strenuous outing could justifiably be made into two separate day-trips with an overnight spent at the Mont Fort hut. But for those who enjoy the challenge of a very full mountain day, advice is to start as early as possible to allow sufficient time during the walk to enjoy indolent moments with big views. Keep alert, too, for the possible sighting of chamois and even ibex along the way.

Follow directions to the Cabane du Mont Fort as outlined in Route 71. From the hut head east to join a path that breaks away to the right from the Col des Gentianes track to swing slightly west of south round the slopes of Bec des Rosses. Passing round the shoulder of the mountain you enter the steep but shallow southern cirque of Bec des Rosses with the valley floor more than fifteen hundred metres below. The path crosses round the cirque, is joined by another, and comes to Col Termin 5½ hours after leaving Verbier (2½ hours from Cabane du Mont Fort). Below to the east lies Lac de Louvie.

The way forks. Both routes lead down to Alp de Louvie with its tarn in an idyllic setting, with lovely views across the valley to the Grand Combin. The left-hand trail traverses into the rough Louvie corrie; the right-hand path goes along the shoulder of mountain before cutting down to the water's edge. From the southern end of the tarn the continuing path heads alongside the stream which drains it, passes some alp huts and then drops steeply down the hillside in numerous tiring zig-zags to reach Fionnay.

Route 73: **Fionnay (1,490m)-Cabane de Pannoissière (2,669m)**

Grade: 3
Distance: 7kms
Height gain: 1,179 metres
Time: 4 hours

One of the principal features of this route is the dramatic contrast it affords between the valley scenery of Fionnay and that which is revealed from the Pannossière hut. It is an exchange of soft grassland for the arctic savagery of snowfield and glacier, while the icy cataracts that hang suspended from the north face of Grand Combin bear witness to a world as yet resistant to the tender mercy of vegetation. It's a lovely, yet raw, sense of majesty; a heartland of big shapely peaks, of lofty mountain walls and a long stretch of glacier. Our path leads right to the edge of this heartland, thus enabling the walker to gain an insight of the sculptor of this mountain world at work: the sculptor whose tool is ice.

From Fionnay cross to the left bank of the Druce and take the path leading from the southern shore of the tarn heading south-west and rising steadily towards the opening of the narrow Corbassière valley. Soon wind up in zig-zags to make height. The path is met by another rising from the right (1,818m), and then climbs on to traverse round the end wall of mountain. Once round the bluff the route swings south to pass a line of five small chalets delightfully set above a former glacier bed. The views from here grow ever more spectacular as you gaze across the tongue of the Corbassière ice-field to the Petit Combin, then the pyramid of Combin de Corbassière on its shoulder, and to the Grand Combin itself at the head of the valley.

The footpath now traverses roughly southward along a more-or-less level section and enters Plan Goli. At the end of this you climb steeply by way of more tight zig-zags, then swing left to follow along the edge of the glacier all the way to the hut *(refreshments)* which is found among the moraines on the right bank. (To return to Fionnay along the same path, allow 2½ hours.)

Above Cabane de Pannossière to the north-east lies the Col des Otanes. A path climbs over this as a convenient breach in the high mountain wall below Grand Tavé, and a descent from here makes an interesting alternative route back to the Val de Bagnes. Some way below the north-east of the col the path forks, allowing one route to drop steeply into the valley bed at Bonatchesse, while the right-hand branch traverses round the mountainside to Mauvoisin. The Postbus runs from here back to Fionnay.

Other Routes from Fionnay:
Practically all the walks from Fionnay start with a steep ascent of the walling hillsides. **ALP de LOUVIE** (2,215m 2 hours) will always be worth the effort involved in reaching it because of its splendid views. Try also linking a number of small alps on the north-eastern side of the

valley. First go up to Lac de Louvie, then follow a path heading east to Le Dâ (2,365m), then south to cross the little ridge of Tête du Sarclay to gain Ecurie du Crêt (2,298m). From here the path traverses easily along to Ecurie du Vasevay (2,155m) before slanting down into the valley just outside Bonatchesse.

There's a long and strenuous crossing to be made of **COL de LOUVIE** (2,921m) from Fionnay. This would lead the energetic walker into Val de Nendaz. (Allow 8 hours from Fionnay to Haute Nendaz.)

The ascent of **ROSABLANCHE** (3,336m) is also a practical proposition for experienced mountain walkers based on Fionnay. A five-hour outing, the route climbs steeply above the village to the alp pastures of Le Dâ, and from there up to Col de Cleuson (3,018m) on the north-west ridge of Rosablanche. From the col to the summit the way follows this ridge without difficulty in about one hour.

Route 74: Mauvoisin (1,841m)-Lacs de Tsofeiret (2,572m)-Cabane de Chanrion (2,462m)

Grade:	2		
Distance:	10kms		
Height gain:	801 metres	**Height loss:**	180 metres
Time:	4 hours		

Cabane de Chanrion is a popular hut with climbers, long distance walkers and with all who fancy an undemanding day's wandering among fine mountain scenery. It makes an obvious goal for an outing, and when linked with a visit to the trio of tarns of Tsofeiret to the north, an added dimension is given. Views are quite delightful. There's the possibility of catching sight of chamois or marmots, and in early summer there will be masses of wild flowers.

Either take the Postbus to Mauvoisin or park just outside the hamlet near the huge dam. Follow the road to the head of the barrage and walk across it to the eastern side. From here a rough track heads alongside the lake and goes through one or two tunnels. Above curls the Glacier du Giètro from La Ruinette and Mont Blanc de Cheilon, its streams pouring down on bright summer days to form cascades. After a while the track gains height by climbing the hillside in long twists, and is then replaced by a marked footpath heading south and crossing several streams. Views across the valley are to the east face of Grand Combin, while ahead rises Point d'Otemma (3,403m) below which sits the Chanrion hut.

In a little over three hours from Mauvoisin the path leads to the Lacs de Tsofeiret set among pastures from which one gains striking views of Grand Combin. Continue along the footpath which goes up to a low crest, and then descend over screes below the long and narrow Glacier du Brenay that comes from Pigne d'Arolla. Beyond the screes the route is straightforward. It leads directly to the hut *(refreshments)*. Cabane de Chanrion is also set near tarns, and with its amphitheatre of peaks wearing little glacial napkins to the south, its views to Grand Combin, and the opportunity to return to Mauvoisin by way of an easy track along the west bank of Lac de Mauvoisin - thus making a loop trip - this route is highly recommended.

Note: To the south-west of the hut, between Mont Avril and Mont Gelé, lies the easy pass of Fenêtre de Durand (2,797m) - a noted site for alpine plants - which forms the Swiss/Italian border. This is one of the outings made easily accessible from a base at the hut, while a crossing of the pass gives an opportunity to descend to the lovely Valpelline or, without dropping that far, traversing round the mountainside heading roughly west in order to regain entry to Switzerland over one of the cols neighbouring the Grand St. Bernard at the head of Val d'Entremont. Such an expedition may be used as part of a circuit of the Grand Combin massif. (See Route 88.)

VAL d'ENTREMONT

Position:	**South of the Rhône, and reached from Martigny via Val de Bagnes.**
Map:	**L.S. 5003 'Mont Blanc-Grand Combin' 1:50,000**
Bases:	**Orsières (901m) Liddes (1,346m) Bourg St. Pierre (1,632m)**
Tourist Information:	**Office du Tourisme, 1937 Orsières (Tel: 026 4 1531) Office du Tourisme, 1931 Liddes (Tel: 026 4 2988) Office du Tourisme, 1932 Bourg St. Pierre (Tel: 026 4 9141)**

Because of the comparative ease and accessibility of the Col du Grand St. Bernard at its head, the Val d'Entremont has seen a steady procession of travellers through its bright sloping pastures for many centuries. It was known to the Celts and to the Romans. Emperors and armies marched this way, and countless religious pilgrims have made the journey to Rome along the valley and over its historic pass. In the 11th century a hospice was founded at the pass, and in the winter of 1178 a fearful English monk, John de Bremble, reached the Grand St. Bernard uttering the prayer: 'Lord restore me to my brethren that I may tell them that they shall not come to this place of torment.'

In summer the valley is green and pleasant. There are few settlements and those, fortunately, have now been by-passed by the busy modern road that goes up to the St. Bernard. It begins at Sembrancher in the lower reaches of Val de Bagnes, a south-projecting valley that forks again at Orsières where the Val Ferret continues ahead while that of Entremont veers south-eastwards. Some 8 kilometres or so from Orsières the village of Liddes stands well above the river on its gentle slope of grassland with woods backing it and a side road branching away towards Chandonne. Six kilometres farther along the valley and the road climbs above Bourg St. Pierre, a small mountaineering centre noted for its alpine garden. Above to the east rise the aiguilles of Maisons Blanches, outliers of the Grand Combin, while Mont Vélan (3,731m) forms a bold signature to the south-east.

Continuing beyond Bourg St. Pierre the road eases and runs along the shore of Lac des Toules, which is yet another of the many reservoirs that lie in these southern valleys of Canton Valais. At the far end of the reservoir, at a height of 1,915 metres, the road forks. At this point we come to the entrance to a toll tunnel, almost 6 kilometres long, which was completed in 1964 and which burrows beneath the mountains blocking the upper end of the valley. This tunnel emerges at a height of 1,875 metres on the Italian side of the frontier, while the older traditional road continues to climb by way of a series of hairpins to reach the Grand St. Bernard Pass (2,469m) with its massive stone buildings, its little lake, its museum and monuments and dogs.

Valley Bases:
ORSIÈRES (901m) lies below the St. Bernard road at the junction of Val d'Entremont and Val Ferret, a busy little town at the end of a branch railway line coming up from Martigny. In addition to being conveniently situated for walks in either of the main valleys cutting away from it, Orsières also guards access to the road which climbs up to Champex and the little Val d'Arpette. In the town there are various shops, banks, restaurants and small hotels, and a tourist information office.
LIDDES (1,346m) is a village with the air of a pastoral community. It occupies a meadowland site above the main road, with accommodation to be had in four hotels. From it roads lead north along the hillside to the small village of Chandonne, and down to the valley bed where the hamlet of Drance is found.
BOURG ST. PIERRE (1,632m) is an historic village with some lovely old buildings including a Romanesque church tower and a milestone dating from Roman times. In May 1800 Napoleon came through the valley with 40,000 men on his way to Italy, each regiment taking three days to cross the pass, and each one staying overnight in Bourg St. Pierre prior to making the passage of the Grand St. Bernard. Several hotels and dormitories offer assorted accommodation. There is a tourist information office to help with enquiries.

Mountain Huts:
There are two SAC huts accessible from Val d'Entremont, both reached by way of paths leading from Bourg St. Pierre. **CABANE de VALSOREY** (3,030m) stands high upon the south-western slopes of Grand Combin de Valsorey on a perch of rock overlooking Mont

Vélan. It's a small hut, by standards of SAC accommodation found elsewhere in the Valais, with only spaces for 36 in its dormitories. It has no permanent guardian in charge. The route to it involves something of a scramble (chain assisted) and takes 4½-5 hours from Bourg St. Pierre.

CABANE du VÉLAN (2,569m) is larger than its neighbour, having room for 55. It stands to the north of Mont Vélan with magnificent views up to its lovely ice-topped face, and across to the Grand Combin. The hut has a guardian in residence during summer, when meals and drinks are available. The path to it from Bourg St. Pierre will take about 3 hours.

Route 75:   **Orsières (901m)-Bourg St. Pierre (1,632m)**

Grade: 1-2
Distance: 13kms
Height gain: 731 metres
Time: 3½ hours

This is an undemanding walk that follows the course of the Drance d'Entremont upstream through pastures and along the edge of woods on a waymarked trail. For those with sufficient energy the route could be continued all the way to the Grand St. Bernard, but this would require about seven hours of walking.

Find the road that leads south out of Orsières to join the main valley road heading to the Grand St. Bernard, but before it actually joins the main road cut away from it on a track to the right. This goes across the river to the south and then heads uphill among trees to reach the few chalets of Montatuay (1,062m). From here bear left and continue along the track to the hamlet of Fornex (1,216m) where the way divides. Go through Fornex and take the middle of three paths which will lead through the forest for a little under 2 kilometres when you cross a side-stream near Pont de la Tsi (which leads over the main river). Continue on the true left bank of the Drance d'Entremont (west side) to reach the little village of Drance (1,255m). A track continues beside the river enjoying its company all the way to a point a little south of Bourg St. Pierre where you may cross to the right bank and climb up to the village. (About 1.5 kilometres before reaching the village a narrow road crosses the river and also goes up to Bourg St. Pierre. Either route will do.) Catch the Postbus back to Orsières.

Route 76:   **Liddes (1,346m)-Tour de Bavon (2,476m)**

Grade: **2-3**
Distance: **7kms**
Height gain: 1,221 metres   Height loss: 91 metres
Time: **3½ hours**

West of Val d'Entremont runs the pasture-smooth Val Ferret, and between the two a long spine of modestly-proportioned mountain projects northward from the frontier ridge overlooking the Grand St. Bernard. That northward projection is, in itself, divided with the Combe de l'A making a neat vale between. Below Liddes the hamlet of Drance guards the entrance to the Combe de l'A, and this walk takes us across the combe's opening and up onto the crest of the ridge which makes a wall between it and the Val Ferret. Tour de Bavon is a viewpoint of great character. Not only does it survey the deep cut of both the Vals d'Entremont and Ferret, but it gazes south-west to Mont Blanc and its fabulous aiguilles, and south-east to the Grand Combin and Mont Vélan.

From Liddes descend by road to Drance on the left bank of the river. Immediately one has a choice to make. Either a) bear right and walk along the road to Vicheres (1,423m), and from there continue with the road as it climbs in long sweeps through forest up the hillside, or b) walk through Drance and follow the narrow road which swings up the sloping pastures to Chez Petit (1,365m), at which point break away along a track going to the right along the edge of forest towards the northern bluff of mountain marked as Cornet (1,465m) on the map.

If following route a) the road leads to an open alp pasture called Le Chapelet (1,642m). A track then continues to sweep through forest gaining height until it comes to the open pastures of Bavon (2,030m).

Route b) cuts away to the south-west from Cornet (take the left-hand of two paths round into the Combe de l'A), crosses the Torrent de l'A and climbs through forest to Les Torrents and up to Bavon (about 2½ hours).

From Bavon head west up the slope to gain the crest of Le Tessure at point 2,267m in about half an hour, then bear left to wander along the easy ridge for a further half-hour to reach the crown of Tour de Bavon and its superb views. (Allow 2½ hours for the return to Liddes.)

An alternative descent could be made into Val Ferret. Return down the ridge to point 2,267m where you will find a path heading south-west down the Ferret slope. This leads soon to the alp of La Sasse (1,970m) where the path forks. Take the right branch heading north. It leads down through forest to the valley at Praz de Fort (1,151m 2½ hours from the ridge; total 6 hours from Liddes) from where you can catch a Postbus to Orsières, and another from there to Liddes.

Other Routes from Liddes:
Liddes gives access to a number of pastoral outings that are ideal for the 'middle-ranks' of mountain walkers, that is to say those for whom the rugged high passes are out of bounds, but who gain much pleasure from wandering through pastures and forest and across moderate ridges. Certainly the views to be had from some of these outings are in no way second-rate, and a few are actually superior to those gained from some of the more remote summits. On some of these walks there are possibilities of seeing deer or chamois or marmots, and in late spring and early summer the meadows are bright with an extravagant flora.

Two routes lead into or through the lovely **COMBE de l'A** which juts southward from the hamlet of Drance. The first, a long one, goes all the way through to cross Col du Néve de la Rousse at its head, and then descends to Ferret, the last hamlet in Val Ferret (accommodation, Postbus etc.). The other wanders halfway into the little valley to the alp of La Tsissette (205m), and about 700 metres beyond it crosses the stream and works its way back along the eastern hillside, crosses over the ridge a little north of Crêta de Vella, and heads off to Bourg St. Pierre by way of La Niord. This outing would take about 5½ hours.

Another lengthy hillside walk of about 6 hours goes north along the mountains that divide Val d'Entremont from Val de Bagnes. Remaining high above the valley the path heads across pastures and through forest, linking one or two alps, to descend into Val de Bagnes at **Le CHÂBLE**.

Yet another walk could be created by following a track that swings up through forest above the village to reach the pastures of La Chaux, then head southward on a high-level traverse of the mountainside from one alp to another before sloping down to **BOURG ST. PIERRE**.

Route 77: **Bourg St. Pierre (1,632m)-**
Cabane de Valsorey (3,030m)

Grade: 3
Distance: 8kms
Height gain: 1,398 metres
Time: 4½-5 hours

The Valsorey is an interesting, rugged little combe that opens to a cirque of peak and glacier whose topmost ridges form the Swiss/Italian border. The 'gateway' to this cirque lies just beyond the Chalets d'Amont from which point one looks up at the tongue of the Glacier de Valsorey ahead, and to that of the Tseudet to the right. Above the Tseudet glacier rises Petit Vélan (3,201m), while to the left the cliffs of Les Botseresses (3,260m) mark the western extremity of the Grand Combin massif. High up ahead to the left the Cabane de Valsorey is tucked beneath the line of cliffs that runs from Les Botseresses to Combin du Meitin, and from it a huge view opens out.

This approach is a taxing one, enlivened by a section involving a chain-aided scramble over an overhang. Anyone unhappy with prospects of reversing such a move should not set out for the hut, but perhaps should content themselves either with the walk to Cabane du Vélan (Route 78), or merely as far as the Chalets d'Amont - which makes a respectable goal on its own.

Go up to the main valley road above Bourg St. Pierre and take the narrow farm road which swings up the hillside above the main highway. When this narrow road ends at a farm, continue along a track heading into the Valsorey some way above the stream. The track becomes a path and there are one or two streams to cross, then at 2,040 metres the path forks. That which heads off to the right goes up to the Cabane du Vélan, but ours, the left branch, climbs ahead up to the Chalets d'Amont (2,197m) in a grand setting. The route forks again, but the two paths rejoin soon after. The path grows steeper and becomes something of a scramble with the chain-assisted overhang to contend with. Above this section the way becomes easier once more, but on the final haul to the hut, the gradient becomes more severe. Note that there is no permanent guardian in charge here, so be prepared to provide all your own meals if you plan to stay overnight. (Allow about two and a half hours for the descent to Bourg St. Pierre.)

Route 78: **Bourg St. Pierre (1,632m)-**
Cabane du Vélan (2,569m)

Grade: **2-3**
Distance: **7kms**
Height gain: **937 metres**
Time: **3 hours**

An easier and more popular hut approach than that to Cabane de Valsorey, this is a highly recommended outing. The walk-in is most agreeable and the views from the hut are delightful.

Follow directions as for Route 77 as far as the path division at 2,040 metres. Bear right and cross the Valsorey torrent on a bridge, and take the clear path which climbs the grassy slope in a series of zig-zags and leads directly to the hut. As you approach, the hut is silhouetted against the huge face of Mont Vélan; a dramatic vision.

In the Val Ferret below La Fouly

VAL FERRET

Position:	**South of the Rhône, and reached from Martigny via Vals de Bagnes and d'Entremont.**
Map:	**L.S. 5003 'Mont Blanc-Grand Combin' 1:50,000**
Bases:	**Orsières (901m) La Fouly (1,592m) Ferret (1,700m)**
Tourist Information:	**Office du Tourisme, 1937 Orsières (Tel: 026 4 1531) Office du Tourisme, 1931 La Fouly (Tel: 026 4 2717)**

A green and gentle land is the Val Ferret. It has the neat orderliness for which Switzerland is noted; its pastures grazed by bell-clattering cattle, its meadows closely mown. Its chalets and hay barns exude an air of peace and well-being. There is an unhurried calm that hangs over forest and grassland alike, yet forming its western wall are the gaunt northern-most ramparts of the Mont Blanc massif: Mont Dolent (3,820m), Tour Noir (3,836m), the Aiguilles of Argentière and Chardonnet, the Grande Fourche and the Aiguilles Dorées - a lofty ridge punctuated by noble peaks and hung about with glaciers.

At the head of the valley Switzerland, Italy and France meet on the summit of Mont Dolent. Below it to the south-east the twin passes of Petit and Grand Cols Ferret (2,490m and 2,537m) link the Swiss Val Ferret with the Italian valley of the same name, and are crossed by that classic alpine long-distance walk, the Tour of Mont Blanc.

Val Ferret is a short and distinctly pastoral valley. From Orsières to the hamlet of Ferret at the end of the road is a distance of only 15 kilometres, but in that brief stretch there's a difference in altitude of almost six hundred metres. The valley rises in steps with pastures open to the sun and forests hugging their borders. To the west rise those outliers of Mont Blanc, to the east the ridge that divides Ferret from Entremont, to the south a modest ridge holding Italy at bay.

Its villages are small, seemingly half-forgotten. Little more than two kilometres from Orsières lies Som la Proz through which the road climbs in a tangle of hairpins to Champex and the little Val d'Arpette. South of Som la Proz we come to Issert astride the road, then Les Arlaches seen as a string of chalets on the right bank of the river. At Praz de Fort the road crosses the river and gives a view west to the snout of the Saleina glacier. Then a smattering of tiny hamlets are found among the pastures until we come to La Fouly, a small village desperately attempting to become an all-year resort. Its position is splendid at the mouth of the cirque of l'A Neuve, gazing up at the glaciers and high ridges topped by the granite tower of the Tour Noir, first climbed from here by the French-born (but naturalized Swiss), Emile Javelle. Outside La Fouly the main valley swings to the south-east, while the so-called Combe des Fonds - marked by a long moraine wall - continues towards the south-west with the Petit Col Ferret at its head. Two kilometres beyond La Fouly stands the little hamlet of Ferret. Beyond the few chalets that comprise this tiny settlement the valley is hidden by the last patch of forest, but long-used tracks head up to a variety of passes that lead into the Italian valleys of Ferret and Grand San Bernardo.

Val Ferret offers some pleasant walks. Some are extremely strenuous, climbing steeply through the narrow shaft of a side-valley or going up to one of the huts perched high above. But some have a more fitting, more gentle quality about them, for they tread soft meadowlands that lead to easy passes from which one breathes the air of distance and gazes off to the great peaks that help raise this corner of the Alps into the realms of enchantment.

Valley Bases:
ORSIÈRES (901m) lies at the junction of Val Ferret and Val d'Entremont at the end of a branch railway line coming up from Martigny. A busy little town with the best shopping facilities available for visitors to Val Ferret. It also has banks, Post Office, restaurants, several small hotels and a tourist information office.
LA FOULY (1,592m) is a good centre for walks and climbs in the area. Although small, it is growing at present into a 'resort' with one or two ski tows on the eastern slopes above the village. A few small hotels with dormitory accommodation as well as standard bedrooms, a campsite on the left bank of the river, restaurants, Post Office and tourist information office. There is also a mountain guides' bureau.
FERRET (1,700m) makes a quiet base at the end of the road. It has limited hotel accommodation and a *pension* offering dormitory accommodation for groups. There is also a restaurant.

Other Valley Bases:
One or two of the valley's other hamlets have limited accommodation for holiday makers. **PRAZ DE FORT** has a hotel-pension with additional dormitory accommodation; also a restaurant. There are restaurants in **BRANCHE** and **PRAYON**, and at **ISSERT**. Food stores will be found at La Fouly, Praz de Fort and Issert.

The valley is regularly served in summer by Postbus from Orsières to Ferret, but note that the number of daily journeys changes from month to month between May and October.

Mountain Huts:
Apart from a small bivouac hut perched on the east ridge of Mont Dolent, the SAC has four huts accessible from Val Ferret. **CABANE d'ORNY** (2,811m) lies below Pointe d'Orny on the north bank of the glacier of the same name. With places for 80 and a guardian in occupation between June 20th and mid-September each year, when meals will be available, this is a popular lodging. There are several routes to it, the shortest being by way of chair-lift from Champex to La Breya followed by a two-hour walk. It is also accessible from Praz de Fort via Plan Bagnet and the crossing of the Chevrettes ridge, and from Orsières by way of the Combe d'Orny in about 5½ hours.

Neighbouring Cabane d'Orny above the glacier pass linking the Orny glacier with the Plateau du Trient, **CABANE du TRIENT** (3,170m) has room for 155 in its dormitories. A number of ascents are made possible by using this hut as a base, as well as several interesting glacier tours. There is a guardian in residence from mid-June to mid-September providing meals and drinks. The hut is reached by way of the glacier above Cabane d'Orny in about one hour.

CABANE de SALEINA (2,691m), as its name suggests, is found near the Saleina glacier in full view of the cirque created by such splendid peaks as Aiguille d'Argentière, Aiguille du Chardonnet and the Grande Fourche. Provided by the Section Neuchâteloise, the hut can sleep 43. It has a guardian for a short summer period only, between July 10th and August 31st. Meals are not provided, but drinks are usually available. The approach from Praz de Fort will take about 4½ hours.

Above La Fouly, from which village it is approached in about 3½ hours, **CABANE da l'A NEUVE** (2,735m) makes a base for climbs on the Aiguilles Rouges du Dolent, Mont Dolent, Tour Noir, Grande Lui and many more. It's only a small hut with places for 26. The guardian is in occupation usually between the beginning of July and the middle of September, and then meals and drinks will be available.

Route 79: **Praz de Fort (1,151m)-Plan Bagnet (1,770m)-Cabane d'Orny (2,811m)**

Grade:	**3**
Distance:	**7kms**
Height gain:	**1,660 metres**
Time:	**5½ hours**

This is the main approach to the Orny hut from Val Ferret. It follows a clear path all the way and, although strenuous, should cause no difficulties.

The main valley road forks at the northern entrance to Praz de Fort. Break away from the main road and take that which skirts the western side of the village heading south. On by-passing Praz de Fort it then veers to the right to enter the Saleina glen, a valley that soon becomes very steep with the snout of a glacier seen curling at its head. Follow this road through forest until it becomes a track, and continue until you come to a path which branches off to the right. This climbs the steep mountainside in a series of loops heading north-west below the crest of Pointes des Chevrettes. As you work a way up the path, so views open to the Aiguille d'Argentière (3,876m) and Aiguille du Chardonnet (3,680m) off to the south-west in the cirque blocking the Saleina valley. Towards the top of the slope the path steepens with more zig-zags. Once atop the crest the route swings steadily round to the left to find the hut *(refreshments)* on the north bank of the Glacier d'Orny.

Route 80: **Praz de Fort (1,151m)-Cabane de Saleina (2,691m)**

Grade:	**3**
Distance:	**6kms**
Height gain:	**1,540 metres**
Time:	**4½ hours**

Originally built in 1893 the Saleina hut stands in a wonderful cirque of high mountains adorned by a great ice-field. Above rise staggering peaks broken here and there by historic passes that lead over the ridges and into France. It is a fabulous position in which to spend a starlit night and to watch daylight creep in. And the approach to it is ever-interesting, leading as it does through various zones of vegetation, giving opportunities to study glacial moraines, the buckled distortions of the glacier itself, fine peaks and splendid views. Where the route demands, chains have been fixed to aid the laden walker over one or two sections.

Follow directions as for Route 79 as far as the end of the road leading into the Saleina glen. As the road ends a path breaks away to the right, waymarked for the cabane. It crosses the Reuse de Saleina (glacial torrent) and heads upstream, along the glacial moraine, winds round the towering rocks of Clochers des Planereuses (2,806m) and climbs on to reach the hut. *(Drinks only may be available at the hut.)* Allow about 3 hours for the descent to Praz de Fort.

Route 81: La Fouly (1,592m)-Cabane de l'A Neuve (2,735m)

Grade:	3
Distance:	5kms
Height gain:	1,143 metres
Time:	3½-4 hours

This very steep hut approach takes the walker out of the soft green valley and up to a raw landscape of rock and ice. A strenuous but interesting outing. Cabane de l'A Neuve, incidentally, is otherwise known as Cabane Dufour. It has a fine view of the ice-bound north face of Mont Dolent across the cirque.

Take the campsite approach track leading down from the valley road in La Fouly to pass the guides' bureau and bear right beside several chalets set among trees. Follow the track across the river to the undulating meadows of the village campsite, and from there continue ahead on a rough path (paint flashes) leading among trees and shrubs into the glen topped by the Tour Noir and Aiguilles Rouges. The path leads steeply up the moraine rib on the northern side of the valley (true left bank) with the blunt snout of the Glacier de l'A Neuve seen off to your left. The path crosses one of the glacial streams and then steepens with numerous tight zig-zags to gain the hut. *(Refreshments available.)*

Route 82: Ferret (1,700m)-Grand Col Ferret (2,537m)

Grade:	2
Distance:	6kms
Height gain:	837 metres
Time:	2 hours 45 mins

The pass of the Grand Col Ferret is a much-frequented one, especially so since it is on the route of the classic Tour of Mont Blanc. From it one has splendid views to enjoy, and an easy day could be well spent in wandering to it under a bright sky, having a picnic nearby, and taking a leisurely stroll back again. For those inclined to lengthen the walk, or to whom a night in Italy appeals, a descent into the Italian Val Ferret could easily be accomplished.

The motor road extends for another kilometre or so to the south of Ferret, and from its end a choice of tracks is given. Take the right-hand branch to cross the water of the Drance, and climb with it in long sweeps to the south to reach the alp of La Peule (2,071m). A path leads gently on from here heading west, and goes all the way to the pass.

Views from the vicinity of the Grand Col Ferret extend through the Italian Val Ferret to the Val Veni beyond with the Col de la Seigne at its head, some thirty kilometres away. To the west rise the powerful shapes of the Grandes Jorasses and Aiguille du Géant blocking the higher snows of Mont Blanc. Nearer to hand the ridge rises to Mont Dolent, while to the north-east can be seen the Grand Combin and Mont Vélan.

If returning to Ferret, allow about 1½-2 hours by the same path.

Route 83: Ferret (1,700m)-Lacs de Fenêtre (2,456m 2,495m)-Fenêtre de Ferret (2,698m)

Grade:	2
Distance:	8kms
Height gain:	998 metres
Time:	3 hours

The scant pastures that surround the Lacs de Fenêtre make a great place for a picnic. From them one gains lovely views across the contortions of this upper valley to the cone of Mont Dolent and so many grand peaks, including that of the Grandes Jorasses; a view that encompasses a high landscape dominated by rock and snow and ice. On calm, clear summer days this is an idyllic place to spend an hour or so in idle contemplation, but if the wind is blowing down in the valley, stay away from these upper pastures and turn your attention elsewhere.

Wander up-valley out of Ferret as far as the end of the road, then continue ahead on the track which remains on the right bank of the stream (north-east side) climbing above a narrow rocky gorge. Halfway along this gorge the track forks. Take the left-hand branch that goes up to the alp hut of Les Ars-Dessus (1,955m). Another path breaks away here to climb steeply to the col which leads into the Combe de l'A (see Val d'Entremont section). Ignore this option and continue on the main track which swings to the south and climbs in more loops to reach the buildings of Plan de la Chaux (2,041m).

Again the way divides. Our path now breaks away to the left, climbing still up the hillside, steepening in zig-zags before coming to the first of the tarns. Once more the path forks. Our route lies in going south along the western shore of the tarn, while the alternative path climbs north then east to cross Col du Bastillon immediately below the converging ridges of Monts Telliers. Our path continues to gain height towards the south over grassy bluffs between two further tarns, and soon after emerges onto the pass of Fenêtre de Ferret above the Col du Grand St. Bernard.

Val d'Arpette

VAL d'ARPETTE

Position:	**West of Val d'Entremont, and reached by way of Orsières.**
Map:	**O.S. 5003 'Mont Blanc-Grand Combin' 1:50,000**
Base:	**Champex (1,466m)**
Tourist Information:	**Office du Tourisme, 1938 Champex-Lac (Tel: 026 4 1227)**

Val d'Arpette is tucked away as a vale of seclusion, often ignored by visitors to the Valais since it is rather off the regular route of holiday-makers. And yet it has been known since the earliest days of Mont Blanc's exploration, and even in Victorian times there were sufficient British visitors to Champex that during the summer months English church services were conducted there.

It's a small valley cradled by the outstretched arms of ridges projecting north-eastwards from Pointe d'Orny and Pointe des Ecandies. On the northern shoulder of the latter the pass of Fenêtre d'Arpette (2,665m) leads over to the Glacier du Trient, northern-most ice-sheet of the Mont Blanc massif. The lower portion of the valley is green and soft and luxuriously vegetated; its upper regions are barren, stony, scree-laden. The contrasts are substantial.

Walking in this little valley can be as gentle or as strenuous as you wish. There are easy forest or lakeside walks, and there are energetic outings that lead across the surrounding ridges. The classic Tour of Mont Blanc comes this way with a choice of routes between Champex and Trient; either crossing Fenêtre d'Arpette, or the so-called Bovine route via the forests and pastures of Bovine alp to La Forclaz.

Champex itself, the only village in the valley, is an attractive lake-side resort on a green and wooded plateau, reached by way of a steeply climbing hairpin road from Orsières at the junction of Val Ferret and Val d'Entremont, or from the north by another steeply-twisting road which leaves the mouth of Val de Bagnes at Les Valettes. The village is served by Postbus from Orsières, which itself is reached by train from Martigny.

Valley Base:
CHAMPEX (1,466m), sometimes known as Champex-Lac as if to emphasize its lakeside position, has been eagerly developed as an all-year resort. There is boating and fishing in the lake, dancing, tennis, swimming in a heated pool, and an alpine garden (*Jardin alpin Florealpe*) containing more than 4,000 plants. There should be no difficulty experienced in finding suitable accommodation, for Champex has a number of hotels and *pensions*, some containing dormitories for those travelling on a restricted budget, a Youth Hostel (*Auberge de Jeunesse*) and a campsite. There are also several chalets and apartments to rent. The village has assorted shops, banks, Post Office, restaurants and a tourist information bureau.

Mountain Huts:
Two SAC huts are accessible from Champex, both using the same approach routes. **CABANE d'ORNY** (2,811m) has places for 80 in its dormitories. There is a guardian in residence between June 20th and mid-September, when meals will be available. The hut sits on the northern bank of the Orny glacier, and is reached either by path from the chalets of Arpette crossing over Col de la Breya (2,401m), by footpath round the shoulder of La Breya and through the Combe d'Orny, or by chair-lift to La Breya (2,188m) followed by footpath into the Combe d'Orny. This is the shortest route and it takes about 2 hours from the chair-lift.
CABANE du TRIENT (3,170m) stands about an hour above Cabane d'Orny overlooking the glacier of Plateau du Trient and the Aiguille du Tour. This hut can sleep 155 and has a guardian in residence from mid-June to mid-September when meals are provided. The route to it from the Orny hut leads over the Glacier d'Orny.

Route 84:   Champex (1,466m)-Fenêtre d'Arpette (2,665m)

Grade:	**3**
Distance:	**7kms**
Height gain:	**1,199 metres**
Time:	**3 hours**

This walk is of the more strenuous variety, easy at first, but growing a little more taxing as the pass grows nearer. It is on the route of the Tour of Mont Blanc *Variante*, the ascent section of the stage which leads to Trient, so it will not be unusual to find other walkers heading along the same path on a fine summer's day.

Go round the lake opposite Champex and follow the broad track heading up-valley to pass beneath the chair-lift that goes to La Breya. Continue ahead into the valley proper among woods still, and then alongside the stream to the open pastureland of Arpette (1,627m) with its chalets and barns. *(Refreshments.* Accommodation also available here, including *dortoir.)* The waymarked path continues across the pastures and beside the clear stream, but soon brings you to a rougher terrain. Once the treeline has been deserted the valley becomes stonier, and the path is sometimes a little faint, although waymarkings are there for guidance.

Climbing south-westward the path leads up to the alp of La Barme where it forks. Take the right-hand option, rising among crags and boulders towards the narrow cut of the pass in the ridge ahead; the so-called 'window' of the valley. The boulder field gives way to a tiring slope of gravel (snow early in the season, or following bad weather) that takes you to the pass itself.

From Fenêtre d'Arpette a marvellous panorama is spread before you. Below lies the jumbled sérac-ridden Glacier du Trient, caught in a frozen cascade on its slow-motion journey from the catchment area under the Aiguille du Tour and Aiguilles Dorées. Beyond the Aiguille du Tour rise the savage yet magnificent towers and spires and ridges of the Mont Blanc massif. Behind to the east the Val d'Arpette is laid out for inspection. It's a fair reward for the exercise required to gain this perch.

To return to Champex by the same path will require about two hours, but for those who would continue down to Trient along the Tour of Mont Blanc route, allow 2½ hours for the downhill leg. It is well-marked all the way, if requiring some care initially, and the Trient valley is an attractive one. Keep your camera handy. Return from Trient to Champex by public transport: Postbus to Martigny, train from Martigny to Orsières, Postbus from Orsières to Champex.

Route 85: Champex (1,466m)-Cabane d'Orny (2,811m)

Grade:	**2-3**
Distance:	**6kms**
Height gain:	**1,345 metres**
Time:	**4 hours**

This hut approach offers a mixture of woodland, open valley, glacial slabs and boulders. An interesting walk, it is gentle in places, strenuous in others. Refreshments should be available at the hut.

On the western shore of Lac de Champex stands a white-painted Protestant church. A path leads between it and the lake, and a track runs parallel with this path, but behind the church. Walk along this track heading south-east and when it forks, take the right-hand branch which is waymarked to Combe d'Orny. Follow this steadily through the forest, with paint flashes (white-red-white) being the guide. The path swings round the eastern slopes of La Breya, gaining a little height, and crosses a path descending from the summit. Shortly after this you enter Combe d'Orny and descend to the stream cutting through it.

The path leads alongside the stream a short distance, crosses it and begins to climb among screes and boulders and glacial slabs. For some way the path climbs through the valley above the stream, but then is forced to cross it once more to the true left bank. It is joined by another path coming from both Col de la Breya and the chair-lift at La Breya (the alternative approach routes from Val d'Arpette). Continue up-valley to reach the hut.

Route 86: Champex (1,466m)-Le Bonhomme (2,435m)

Grade:	2
Distance:	4.5kms
Height gain:	969 metres
Time:	3½ hours

The summit of Le Bonhomme (and, to a certain extent, its loftier neighbour Le Catogne) has long been a noted belvedere from which to view the snow and rock peaks of the Mont Blanc massif, and also the great summits of the Pennine Alps to the east - including Monte Rosa and the Matterhorn. A footpath leads all the way to the summit. It's a steep route, but the views will make the effort worthwhile.

At the eastern end of Lac de Champex walk away from the village along the left-hand road (between a café and a boutique) as far as the Alpina restaurant where a footpath heads off to the left, signposted as Chemin du Devin. This leads through forest, gaining height for a little over a kilometre until another path breaks away to the left to climb in steep zig-zags up to the ridge. This is the path to take, and it is waymarked with paint flashes. Crossing the ridge, still among trees, the path swings to the right to wander gently along the western side. When another path joins ours from the left (coming from Champex on a severe course) the route zig-zags steeply once more and emerges above the trees. Rejoining the ridge the path goes up to the summit of

Le Bonhomme where it is tempting to relax at last and soak in the views.

Le Catogne (2,598m) rises to the north beyond the secondary peak of Pointe des Chevrettes (2,568m) and is reached in about 40 minutes from Le Bonhomme. To return to Champex by the same path will take about 2 hours. An alternative descent route continues to the north-west from the summit, losing height gradually until a junction of paths is met. Turn left to drop steeply down to Champex d'en Haut, where you bear left and wander along the road to Champex.

Other Routes from Champex:

A glance at the map will show numerous possibilities for walks in the Val d'Arpette and neighbouring mountains, and the staff at the tourist information office will add other suggestions. There is the 'official' TMB (Tour of Mont Blanc) stage which goes from Champex to La Forclaz - the **BOVINE** route. This is mostly a forest walk that offers extensive views along the Rhône Valley. It goes through the alp hamlet of Bovine (1,987m) about 2 hours from Champex, and reaches La Forclaz in about four hours from the start.

There's a challenging outing that follows Route 85 to Cabane d'Orny, then breaks away to cross the Chevrettes ridge, descends into the **SALEINA GLEN** and joins the Val Ferret at Praz de Fort. From here a return to Champex is made via Issert and a forest path round the slopes of La Breya. This would require about 7½ hours of walking.

From Champex there's a forest-and-meadow path that leads to **SEMBRANCHER** at the junction of Val de Bagnes and Val d'Entremont, linking isolated alp hamlets on the way. This will take about 2½ hours to complete.

A circuit of the lake ought to be made either early in the morning or in the evening to catch the light and to watch the fish jumping. Similarly, a stroll through the woods in early morning will give the opportunity to catch sight of deer - if you move quietly. There will always be plenty to keep an inquisitive mind happy, and enough footpath options and variations to justify a week's holiday based here.

The Moming Glacier seen from the path which leads from Sorebois to Petit Mountet
Lac des Dix, at the head of Val d'Hérémence

MULTI-DAY TOURS

Whilst by far the majority of routes contained in this guide will be used as day walks beginning and ending at a valley base, it will be evident that there are numerous possibilities for linking routes together into multi-day journeys, circuits of mountains, the traverse of individual valleys or a number of valleys by the crossing of accessible passes. There are experienced and energetic mountain trekkers for whom this type of travel is the most rewarding of all: working through a challenging landscape day after day, either backpacking or travelling light and staying in mountain huts or cheap valley *pensions* overnight. Such travel demands a high degree of fitness, an understanding of mountain terrain, a sure knowledge of map and compass work, and a certain amount of luck with regard to the weather - as a prolonged bout of storm can result in several days of frustration if marooned in an isolated hut or a small tent.

For this class of wanderer the following suggested tours are recommended.

Route 87:	**Tour of the Dents du Midi**

Map:	**L.S. 272 'St. Maurice' 1:50,000**
Length:	**3 days (Total walking time: about 19 hours)**
Accommodation:	**Off-site camping, and Cabane de Susanfe (2,102m)**
Start:	**Vérossaz (811m)**
Finish:	**Vérossaz**

Apart from the last few summits of the Jura crest to the north of Lac Léman, the Dents du Midi form the most westerly mountain group in Switzerland. They are limestone mountains, attractive mountains, especially when viewed from the lakeside at Montreux, spattered with summer snow and rising in a lovely wall to the south. Their highest peaks are Haute Cime (3,257m), Doigts (3,210m) and Dent Jaune (3,186m), and from their summits the views are extensive and justifiably famous. Below them to the south lies the Salanfe basin; an

179

enchanting place dominated by the sparkling Lac de Salanfe reservoir. Emile Javelle wrote rapturously about it more than a century ago and it's been popular with walkers ever since.

The circuit of Dents du Midi explores the surrounding valleys in an anti-clockwise tour that will give three days of worthwhile mountain walking. There are two or three passes to cross, and some lovely valleys to wander through. On the second night accommodation is in Cabane de Susanfe, a hut with 100 places and meals usually available during July, August and September when the guardian is in occupation. Begin the tour at Vérossaz, a village reached from St. Maurice, 15 kilometres north of Martigny in the Rhône Valley. The circuit is given in outline only.

Vérossaz (811m)-Les Jours (1,560m)-Signal de Soi (2,054n.)-Bonavau (1,550m)-Cabane de Susanfe (2,494m)-Col de Susanfe (2,494m)-Lac de Salanfe (1,925m)-Col du Jorat (2,210m)-Mex (1,118m)-Vérossaz.

Route 88:	**Tour of the Combins Massif**
Map:	**L.S. 5003 'Mont Blanc-Grand Combin' 1:50,000**
Length:	**7-8 days (Total walking time: about 48 hours)**
Accommodation:	**A combination of SAC huts, hotels and pensions.**
Start:	**Martigny Bourg (499m)**
Finish:	**Martigny Bourg**

By combining a few of the routes already described under the Val de Bagnes and Val d'Entremont sections, together with a number of new routes, a long circuit of the lovely massif of the Grand Combin can be achieved. The route outlined allows a steady approach to be made. It rises from the depths of the Rhône Valley to climb over the mountain ridge and into the green bowl of hillside above Verbier with its far views, and on to the Cabane du Mont Fort. The Grand Combin grows closer on the stage leading to Fionnay, while on the following stage which leads above the Mauvoisin dam to Cabane de Chanrion, a new aspect is given.

Passing to the south of the Combin, we stray across the frontier into Italy before returning to the Swiss Valais at the Col du Grand St. Bernard. Here a choice of routes may be offered. One can either descend through the Val d'Entremont via Bourg St. Pierre, or as suggested here, through the Combe de l'A to Orsières and via

Champex back to Martigny.

There is a wide variety of scenery to enjoy. It's a challenging circuit, and a rewarding one for those who complete it.

Martigny Bourg (449m)-Chemin Dessus (1,122m)-Col des Planches (1,411m)-Col du Lin (1,656m)-Pierre Avoi (2,472m)-Les Ruinettes (2,195m)-**Cabane du Mont Fort (2,470m via Route 71)**-Fionnay (1,490m Route 72)-Mauvoisin (1,841m)-Cabane de Chanrion (2,462m Route 74)-Fenêtre de Durand (2,797m)-Alpes des Thoules (1,892m)-Barasson (1,900m)-St. Rhémy (1,619m)-Col du Grand St. **Bernard (2,469m)-Col des Chevaux (2,714m)-Lacs de Fenêtre** (2,456m)-Col du Néve de la Rousse (2,752m)-Combe de l'A-Vichères (1,423m)-Orsières (901m)-Champex (1,466m)-Le Borgeaud (633m)-Martigny Bourg.

Route 89:	**North-West Valais**

Maps:	**L.S. 272 'St. Maurice' and 273 'Montana' 1:50,000**
Length:	**4 days (Total walking time: about 24 hours)**
Accommodation:	**A combination of mountain hut, hotels and pensions.**
Start:	**Martigny/La Bâtiaz (474m)**
Finish:	**Sion (512m)**

The north-western slopes of the Rhône Valley are rich in vineyards. They're steep slopes, and from them one has some fine vistas of the valley itself with the big snow and ice-capped peaks rising to the south and east. This multi-day walk gives the chance to explore a corner of the Canton that is often ignored by the walking fraternity to whom the better known peaks and valleys to the south form the main attraction of a mountain holiday. The only SAC hut here is Cabane Rambert (2,585m). It can sleep 44, and meals may be available when the guardian is in residence between early July and the middle of September.

Martigny/La Bâtiaz (474m)-Branson (501m)-Chalet Neuf (1,865m)-**Col du Demècre (2,361m)-Petit Pré (2,001m)-Ovronnaz (1,332m)**-Cabane Rambert (2,585m)-Derborence (1,449m)-Sanetsch (2,047m)-Coppet (1,269m)-Chandolin (818m)-Sion (512m).

Route 90:	**Chamonix to Saas Fee (The Walkers' High Route)**

Maps:	**L.S. 5003 'Mont Blanc-Grand Combin' and 5006 'Matterhorn-Mischabel' 1:50,000**
Length:	**12-14 days**
Accommodation:	**Mostly SAC huts; some hotels or pensions.**
Start:	**Chamonix, France (1,040m)**
Finish:	**Saas Fee (1,809m)**

Today, mention of the *haute route* usually means the classic ski-mountaineering tour between Chamonix and Zermatt (or Saas Fee). But this traverse of some of the finest mountain country in all the Alps originated in the 19th century as an exciting summer walking tour. The route then was very much a mountaineer's route. It meant crossing a number of lofty glacier passes, travelling from hut to hut, or from one high alp hamlet to another where no huts existed. It was (and still is) a magnificent challenge, but one that demanded a high degree of mountaineering expertise.

There is, however, an alternative High Route for fit mountain walkers who perhaps do not possess the necessary experience to tackle the original route of the Victorian pioneers, but who nonetheless have a certain competence in big mountain country. This route is a delight. A long and hard route, it has many tiring passes to tackle as it works its way across the grain of the country. Since the traverse runs more or less west to east, and the valleys cut south to north, it will be evident that practically every stage of this High Route is marked either by a steep ascent or descent - usually sufficient of both to demand a high standard of physical fitness from the outset.

Mountain huts are strategically placed along the line of the traverse to ensure that most nights may be spent in one or another of them, but there are occasions when it will be necessary to seek alternative lodging, perhaps in a hotel, private mountain inn or pension. There should be no difficulty in finding suitable accommodation, and as villages are met on a number of days, it will often be possible to restock with supplies.

The route outlined below is merely one option, but there are several alternative passes that could be chosen depending upon the experience and abilities of the party, thus the actual line of the High Route may be varied to suit. Each will require somewhere in the region of two week to complete.

Chamonix (1,040m)-Col de Balme (2,204m)-Trient (1,297m)-La Forclaz (1,526m)-Fenêtre d'Arpette (2,665m)-Champex (1,466m via Route 84 in reverse)-Orsières (901m)-Le Châble (821m)-Verbier (1,490m)-Cabane du Mont Fort (2,457m Route 71)-Col de Louvie (2,921m)-Grand Desert-(2,800m-*glacier*)-Col de Prafleuri (2,965m)-Cabane de Prafleuri (2,624m)-Le Chargeur (2,102m)-Col de Riedmatten (2,919m)-Arolla (1,998m Route 69)-Les Haudères (1,436m)-Evolène (1,371m)-Col de Torrent (2,919m)-Lac de Moiry (2,249m Route 60 in reverse)-Col de Sorebois (2,896m)-Zinal (1,675m Route 59)-Hotel Weisshorn (2,337m Route 48 in reverse)-Meid Pass (2,790m)-Gruben (1,822m)-Augstbordpass (2,894m)-St. Niklaus (1,127m)-Grächen (1,618m)-Saas Fee (1,809m Route 29).

APPENDIX A
Useful Addresses

1: Tourist Information Offices - other than those mentioned elsewhere with regard to specific bases.

Swiss National Tourist Office
Swiss Centre
New Coventry Street
London W1V 8EE

104 South Michigan Avenue
Chicago
Il 60603

608 Fifth Avenue
New York
NY 10020

250 Stockton Street
San Francisco
CA 94108

P.O. Box 215
Commerce Court
Toronto
Ontario
M5L 1E8

Canton Valais Tourist Office:
Union Valaisanne du Tourisme
15 Rue de Lausanne
1951 Sion
Switzerland

2: Useful Addresses in Switzerland:

Schweizer Hotelier-Verein *(Swiss Hotel Association)*
Monbijoustrasse 130
CH 3001 Berne

Schweizer Alpenclub *(Swiss Alpine Club)*
Helvetiaplatz 4
CH 3005 Berne

Schweizerischer Camping und Caravanning-Verband
            (Swiss Camping & Caravanning Association)
Habsburgerstrasse 35
CH 6004 Lucerne

Verband Schweizer Campings *(Swiss Camping Association)*
Im Sydefädeli 40
CH 8037 Zurich

Schweizerischer Bund für Jugendherbergen
            (Swiss Youth Hostels Association)
Postfach 3229
CH 3001 Berne 22

3: Map Suppliers:

McCarta Ltd
122 Kings Cross Road
London WC1X 9DX

Edward Stanford Ltd
12-14 Long Acre
London WC2

The Map Shop
15 High Street
Upton-upon-Severn
Worcs WR8 0HJ

Rand McNally Map Store
10 East 53rd Street
New York
NY

APPENDIX B
Bibliography

1: General Tourist Guides:

Of the many general tourist guides on the market, perhaps the best and most comprehensive is:-

Blue Guide to Switzerland by Ian Robertson (A & C Black, London. W.W. Norton, New York. Published in 1987 (4th edition)).

2: Mountains and Mountaineering:

Countless volumes devoted to the Alps pack the bookshelves. Those containing references of particular interest to visitors to the Valais are listed below. The list is merely a small selection, but there should be plenty of reading contained within it to provide a good background introduction and to whet the appetite for a forthcoming visit.

Scrambles Amongst The Alps by Edward Whymper (John Murray, London - many editions) - 'Scrambles' is the classic volume of mountaineering literature covering Whymper's Alpine campaigns between 1860 and 1865. It contains, of course, the account of the fateful first ascent of the Matterhorn, but much else besides of interest to visitors to the Valais.

Wanderings Among the High Alps by Alfred Wills (Blackwell, London. Latest edition published 1939) - Another record of Victorian adventures with guides on peaks and passes above Zermatt, Saas Fee etc.

Men and the Matterhorn by Gaston Rébuffat (Kaye & Ward, London 1973. O.U.P. New York 1967) - Well-illustrated volume dedicated to the most famous mountain in Europe.

The Mountains of Switzerland by Herbert Maeder (George Allen & Unwin, London 1968) - Large format book with splendid illustrations.

3: Walking:

Backpacking in Alps and Pyrenees by Showell Styles (Gollancz, London 1976) Contains an account of a large section of the Walkers' High Route across the Pennine Alps, from Martigny to Brig.

Walking in the Alps by J.Hubert Walker (Oliver & Boyd, Edinburgh and London 1951) - Long out of print, but available on special order from most libraries, this is perhaps the best and most readable volume of inspiration to mountain walkers. A large section is devoted to the Pennine Alps. Some information is naturally out of date now, but the book is still highly recommended reading.

4: Climbing:

Selected Climbs in the Pennine Alps (3 volumes) by R.G.Collomb (Alpine Club): *East*, *Central* and *West* (available from West Col Productions, Goring, Reading, Berks RG8 9AA, England).

APPENDIX C
Glossary

The following glossary lists a few words likely to be found on maps, in village streets or in foreign-language tourist information leaflets. It's no substitute for a pocket dictionary, but hopefully will be of some use.

German	French	English
Abhang	pente	slope
Alp	haut pâturage	alp
Alpenblume	florealpe	alpine flower
Alpenverein	club alpin	alpine club
Alphütte	cabane, refuge	mountain hut
Auskunft	renseignements	information
Aussichtspunkt	belle vue	viewpoint
Bach	ruisseau	stream
Bäckerei	boulangerie	bakery
Bahnhof	la gare	railway station
Berg	montagne	mountain
Bergführer	guide de montagne	mountain guide
Berggasthaus	hotel en haut	mountain inn

Bergpass	col	pass
Bergschrund	rimaye	crevasse between glacier and rock wall
Bergsteiger	alpiniste	mountaineer
Bergwanderer	grimpeur	mountain walker
Bergweg	chemin de montagne	mountain path
Blatt	feuille	map sheet
Brücke	pont	bridge
Dorf	village	village
Drahtseilbahn	télépherique	cable-car
Ebene	plaine or plan	plain
Feldweg		meadowland path
Fels	rocher	rock wall or slope
Ferienwohnung	appartement de vacances	holiday apartment
Fussweg	sentier or chemin	footpath
Garni		hotel with meals optional
Gasthaus or gasthof	auberge	inn or guest house
Gaststube	salon	common room
Gefährlich	dangereux	dangerous
Gemse	chamois	chamois
Geröllhalde	éboulis	scree
Gipfel	sommet, cime	summit, peak
Gletscher	glacier	glacier
Gletscherspalte	crevasse	crevasse
Gondelbahn	télécabin	gondola lift
Grat	arête	ridge
Grüetzi	bonjour	greetings
Haltestelle	halte de l'autobus	bus stop
Heilbad	bains chauds	spa, hot springs
Hirsch	cervides	red deer
Hoch	haut	high
Höhe	altitude	height
Höhenweg	haute route	high route
Horn	pic	horn, peak
Hügel	colline	hill
Hütte	cabane, refuge	mountain hut
Jugendherberge	auberge de jeunesse	Youth Hostel
Kamm	crête	crest or ridge
Kapelle	chapelle	chapel
Karte	carte	map
Kirche	église	church
Klamm	gorge, ravin	gorge
Kumme	combe	combe or small valley
Landschaft	paysage	landscape

Lawine	avalanche	avalanche
Lebensmittel	épicerie	grocery
Leicht	facile	easy
Links	á gauche	left
Matratzenlager	dortoir	dormitory
Moräne	moraine	moraine
Murmeltier	marmot	marmot
Nebel	brouillard	fog, low cloud, mist
Nord	nord	north
Ober	dessus	upper
Ost	est	east
Pass	col	pass
Pension	pension	simple hotel
Pfad	sentier, chemin	path
Pickel	piolet	ice axe
Quelle	source, fontaine	spring
Rechts	á droite	right
Reh		roe deer
Rucksack	sac à dos	rucksack
Sattel	selle	saddle, pass
Schlafraum	dortoir	bedroom
Schloss	château	castle
Schlucht	ravine, gorge	gorge
Schnee	neige	snow
See	lac	lake
Seil	corde	rope
Seilbahn	télépherique	cable-car
Sesselbahn	télésiège	chair-lift
Stausee	réservoir	reservoir
Steigesen	crampons	crampons
Steinmann	cairn	cairn
Steinschlag	chute de pierres	falling rock
Stunde	heure	hour
Sud	sud	south
Tal	vallée	valley
Tobel	ravin boisé	wooded ravine
Touristenlager	dortoir	dormitory, tourist accommodation
Über	via, par-dessus	via, or over
Unfall	accident	accident
Unterkunft	logement	accommodation
Verkehrsverien	office (bureau) du tourisme	tourist office
Wald	forêt, bois	forest

Wanderweg	sentier, chemin	footpath
Wasser	eau	water
Weide	pâturage	pasture
West	ouest	west
Wildbach	torrent	torrent
Zeltplatz	camping	campsite
Zimmer	chambres	bedroom
- frei		vacancies

ROUTE INDEX

	Route	Grade	Time	Page
1	Bettmeralp-Hohbalm-Bettmeralp	2	3 hours	29
2	Bettmeralp-Kühboden	1	1 hour 15	31
3	Bettmeralp-Märjelensee-Bettmeralp	2	6-7 hours	31
4	Ferden-Fafleralp (Höhenweg)	2	6½-7 hours	38
4a	Lauchernalp-Faldumalp-Ferden	1	3 hours 40	41
4b	Lauchernalp-Fafleralp	1	2½ hours	41
5	Ferden-Niwen	2	4½ hours	41
6	Ferden-Restipass-Leukerbad	2-3	6-7 hours	42
7	Kummenalp-Lötschenpass-Kandersteg	3	6 hours 45	43
8	Fafleralp-Krindeln	2	1½ hours	44
9	Fafleralp-Gugginalp-Fafleralp	1	2 hours 45	44
10	Fafleralp-Petersgrat-Kandersteg	3	11 hours	45
11	Fafleralp-Blatten-Goppenstein	1	3 hours	46
12	Saas Grund-Saas Fee (Kapellenweg)	1	1 hour 15	56
13	Saas Grund-Sengg-Saas Fee	2	1½ hours	56
14	Saas Grund-Gspon (Höhenweg)	2	5 hours	57
15	Kreuzboden-Weissmies Hut	2	45 mins	58
16	Kreuzboden-Triftalp-Saas Grund	2	2½ hours	58
17	Kreuzboden-Saas Almagell (Höhenweg)	2	3½ hours	60
18	Saas Almagell-Zwischbergen Pass-Almagell	3	8-8½ hours	61
19	Saas Almagell-Zwischbergen Pass-Gondo	3	10½ hours	62
20	Saas Almagell-Antrona Pass-Antronapiana	3	8 hours	62
21	Mattmark Dam-Innere Bodmen-Mattmark	1	2 hours	64
22	Mattmark Dam-Monte Moro Pass-Macugnaga	3	6 hours	65
23	Saas Fee-Längfluh	2	3½ hours	65
24	Saas Fee-Mischabel Hut	3	4½ hours	66
25	Felskinn-Britannia Hut-Saas Fee	2	4 hours	67
26	Plattjen-Britannia Hut	2	2 hours	69
27	Plattjen-Hannig (Gemsweg)	2	3½ hours	70
28	Saas Fee-Hannig-Mällig	2	2½ hours	72
29	Grächen-Saas Fee (Höhenweg Balfrin)	2-3	6½ hours	73
30	Randa-Schaliberg-Randa	2	3½ hours	81
31	Täsch-Täsch Hut	2	4 hours	82
32	Zermatt (Sunnegga)-Ober Sattla-Täschalp	2	2½ hours	83

33	Zermatt-Findeln-Grüensee-Zermatt	2	3-3½ hours	84
34	Sunnegga-Fluhalp-Findeln-Zermatt	1-2	2½-3 hours	85
35	Sunnegga-Stellisee-Oberrothorn	2-3	4 hours	86
36	Gornergrat-Riffelberg-Zermatt	1-2	3½ hours	87
37	Riffelalp-Rotenboden	2	2 hours	88
38	Riffelalp-Gorner Glacier- Monte Rosa Hut	3	4½ hours	89
39	Zermatt-Schwarzsee	2	2½ hours	90
40	Schwarzsee-Hörnli Hut	2	2 hours	91
41	Zermatt-Zmutt	1	50 mins	93
42	Zermatt-Zmutt (high path)	2	2 hours	93
43	Zermatt-Schönbiel Hut	2-3	4 hours	94
44	Zermatt-Trift	2	2 hours 15	95
45	Zermatt-Trift-Mettelhorn	3	6 hours	96
46	Zermatt-Trift-Rothorn Hut	3	5 hours	97
47	Zermatt-Höhbalmen-Zermatt	2	7 hours	98
48	St. Luc-Hotel Weisshorn-Zinal	2	5½-6 hours	106
49	St. Luc-Bella Tola	2-3	4½ hours	107
50	Zinal-Petit Mountet	1-2	1 hour 45	109
51	Zinal-Cabane du Mountet	3	5 hours	109
52	Sorebois-Alp La Lé-Zinal	2	4½ hours	111
53	Zinal-Sorebois	2	1½-2 hours	113
54	Zinal-Roc de la Vache-Ar Pitetta- Zinal	2	5 hours	115
55	Zinal-Cabane de Tracuit	3	5 hours	117
56	Zinal-Cabane d'Ar Pitetta	2	4½ hours	117
57	Barrage de Moiry-Lake Circuit	1	1 hour 50	119
58	Barrage de Moiry-Cabane de Moiry	2	2½ hours	120
59	Barrage de Moiry-Col de Sorebois- Zinal	2	4 hours	121
60	Barrage de Moiry-Col de Torrent- Evolène	2	5 hours	122
61	Les Haudères-Col de la Couronne- Moiry Hut	3	5½ hours	129
62	Les Haudères-Col de Bréona- Les Haudères	3	6½-7 hours	130
63	Ferpècle-Bricola-Ferpècle	2	2½ hours	131
64	Les Haudères-Roc Vieux	2	2½ hours	133
65	Arolla-Pra Gra	1-2	1 hour	134
66	Arolla-Cab. des Aig. Rouges- La Gouille	2-3	4 hours	134
67	Arolla-Plan Bertol-Cabane de Bertol	3	4-5 hours	137

68	Arolla-Pas de Chèvres-Cabane des Dix	3	4-4½ hours	138
69	Le Chargeur-Col de Riedmatten-Arolla	2-3	5½ hours	139
70	Super Nendaz-Lac de Cleuson-Super Nendaz	2	4 hours	145
71	Verbier-Cabane du Mont Fort	2	3 hours	151
72	Verbier-Col Termin-Louvie-Fionnay	3	8½ hours	153
73	Fionnay-Cabane de Pannossière	3	4 hours	153
74	Mauvoisin-Tsofeiret-Cabane de Chanrion	2	4 hours	155
75	Orsières-Bourg St. Pierre	1-2	3½ hours	159
76	Liddes-Tour de Bavon	2-3	3½ hours	160
77	Bourg St. Pierre-Cabane de Valsorey	3	4½-5 hours	162
78	Bourg St. Pierre-Cabane du Vélan	2-3	3 hours	163
79	Praz de Fort-Cabane d'Orny	3	5½ hours	168
80	Praz de Fort-Cabane de Saleina	3	4½ hours	168
81	La Fouly-Cabane de l'A Neuve	3	3½-4 hours	169
82	Ferret-Grand Col Ferret	2	2 hours 45	169
83	Ferret-Lacs de Fenêtre-Fenêtre de Ferret	2	3 hours	170
84	Champex-Fenêtre d'Arpette	3	3 hours	174
85	Champex-Cabane d'Orny	2-3	4 hours	175
86	Champex-La Bonhomme	2	3½ hours	176
87	Tour of the Dents du Midi		3 days	179
88	Tour of the Combins Massif		7-8 days	180
89	North-West Valais		4 days	181
90	Chamonix to Saas Fee		12-14 days	182

PRINTED BY CARNMOR PRINT & DESIGN
95/97 LONDON ROAD, PRESTON.

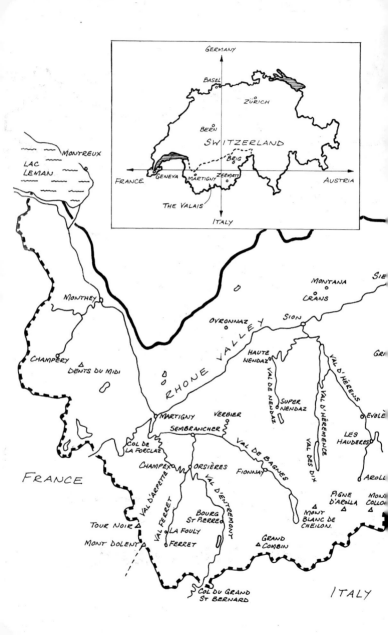